Don't Sweat the Small Stuff

P.S. It's **ALL** Small Stuff

Michael R. Mantell, Ph.D.

Impact Publishers
Post Office Box 1094
San Luis Obispo, California 93406

Library of Congress Cataloging in Publication Data

Mantell, Michael R., 1949-
    Don't sweat the small stuff: P.S., it's all small stuff /
Michael R. Mantell.

    Bibliography: p.
    Includes index.
    ISBN 0-915166-56-9 (pbk.) : $8.95
    1. Conduct of life.   2. Parenting.   3. Health.
    4. Interpersonal relations.   5. Stress (Psychology)
    6. Life change events.
    I. Title.
BF637.C5M34   1988   88- 1596
158 — dc 19   CIP

Publisher's Note

This publication is designed to provide accurate and authoritative information in regard to the subject matter covered. It is sold with the understanding that the publisher is not engaged in rendering psychological, medical, or other professional services. If expert assistance or counseling is needed, the services of a competent professional should be sought.

Credits appear on page 228

Cover design by Emilie Kong, Los Angeles, California
This book is printed on acid-free paper.
Printed in the United States of America

Published by **Impact 𝒮𝒮 Publishers**
POST OFFICE BOX 1094
SAN LUIS OBISPO, CALIFORNIA 93406

Contents

Acknowledgements

This collection of articles represents several years worth of sitting in my study trying to write material that can be easily understood by readers of my columns, while listening to my wife tell our children, "Be quiet while Daddy is writing his newspaper column." To Paula, Benjamin and Jonathan, you can now make some noise, but remember, I have another column due next week! And thanks for your encouragement, understanding, love and especially for putting up with my "mishigas."

I want to acknowledge and thank the best psychology teacher I have ever had, my mother. Though she often reminds us all that she is "*not* a psychologist," her wisdom has always been profound.

As I was organizing my columns for this book, I couldn't help but recall the words of my father who constantly urged me to "write a book." He did not live to see this, and this book is dedicated to his memory and the influence he has had — and continues to have — on my life.

Without Carol and Garry Rosenberg, the publishers of my column, "Ask Dr. Mantell" in their newspaper, the *San Diego Jewish Times,*" this book would not have been possible. I sincerely appreciate my Publisher, Dr. Bob Alberti, for listening to me on the "Bill Ballance Show" and for calling. His hand-holding throughout this process has been invaluable.

My loyal assistant, Paula, (the "other" Paula in my life) has done an outstanding job of assisting me — far beyond anyone's expectations. Her tireless efforts, perhaps more than anyone else's, have helped me actually complete this project.

Finally, I want to give special thanks and appreciation to the readers of my column, my friends, co-workers, and patients for all of their positive feedback and encouragement to share these columns with a wider audience.

Introduction

For a number of years, I've enjoyed the opportunity of writing articles for a variety of publications. I've additionally had the good fortune of dealing with publishers who have allowed me to select my own topics. From the beginning, I've geared my style and subject matter to reach the largest audience I could. Of course, the subject of mental well being concerns all of us, and that's a pretty good-sized audience.

My singular goal in writing these articles has been to offer some guidelines each of us could simply and immediately incorporate into our daily lives. We all have some very basic things in common: ourselves and each other. How we treat ourselves and each other determines our quality of life.

In the past, people may have felt some stigma in seeking professional help with emotional problems. Today, though, the desire to reduce stress, build strong relationships, find job contentment, improve health and obtain a sense of joy in one's life has motivated people to do whatever it takes to reach those goals.

A poet once wrote, "All that we learn, we learn too late, and it's not much." But that's changing even as I sit here. People have gradually learned which questions to ask. They want to know how to deal with their toddlers, their teenagers, their spouses and their health. They're concerned about balancing work and relaxation, they're struggling to redefine relationships with parents and friends. They have been confronted by the complex and sometimes unforgiving future. They're faced with the proliferation of drugs, the spreading of diseases, world terrorism, and violence in their own backyards. They want to know how to handle intimacy and morality, retirement and death. Now they hunger for answers.

Don't Sweat The Small Stuff: P.S. It's All Small Stuff offers a little direction to help you make it through the day.

Part 1.

You

One day a woman came into the office. She was in her early thirties, just divorced after 11 years of marriage. She was very distressed about the direction her life had taken. She hadn't really had to work in over ten years and finding a job was difficult. She couldn't afford her own apartment. Subsequently, she and her five-year-old son had to move back in with her parents. The woman felt she had taken a great step backward in her life. She was sad about her failed marriage and confused about her future. Here she was, after all, back in the room she had grown up in, filled with all its memories of childhood and grand expectations.

After a few days of ruminating in her room, she invited her mother to join her. Her mother sat beside her on the bed.

Her mother asked, "Dolly, what's the matter? You look so depressed. Your father and I don't like to see you so sad."

"Well, Mom," she replied. "My marriage is over. I'm lonely. I'm back where I was 11 years ago. I can't find a job. I don't even know how to look for one. I'm worried about my son, about money. I don't even know who I am."

The mother smiled benevolently and said, "Your father and I just want you to be more cheerful."

The woman told her mother she couldn't be cheerful. She was confused and unhappy. She just wanted to be alone and analyze how she felt about herself, her life, her prospects.

Her mother replied, "Don't think about it if it makes you unhappy. And it's silly to worry about what you're feeling. I never think about sad things and I never worry about what I'm feeling. Just push it all away and you'll feel much better!"

This case history illustrates some old-fashioned thinking coming face-to-face with our fundamental desire to know and understand our innermost feelings. The basic premise of mental wellness today depends on getting in touch with our feelings, allowing ourselves to feel sadness or joy, anger or jealousy.

To meet our own needs, we must know what we need. It seems so simple, yet from an early age we fabricate thick layers between our actions and our feelings, between who we think we are, or should be, and who we really are and how we got there.

Of course, there are reasons for these layers; difficult family and personal relationships, the demands the world places on us to cope in school, on the play yard, in our home and business environment. Change, and our ability to adapt or not adapt, may add protective layers. Everything impacts us, from the competitiveness we feel toward siblings and the give/take relationships we have with our parents, to the stress of everyday life, driving a car, buying groceries, paying bills. What we sometimes lose in the process of living is a true sense of ourselves. What do we feel and why do we feel that way?

The following section focuses on *you*. You can take control of your life, learn who you are and what you're capable of accomplishing. I believe a positive outlook is vital to mental health. I know that sounds easy, but how do you get one of those? Can you buy it at the market? Can you just make a wish and presto, there it is? The truth is, the only way to get one, and to keep it, is through hard work, but the rewards are terrific.

𝕿ips for 𝕷ife's 𝕿rip

Wouldn't life be easy if there were a simple set of rules we could follow that would ensure happiness and satisfaction? Some of you may be thinking, "there already is a set of rules...the Ten Commandments!" Or you may ask, "what about the Golden Rule?"

Inevitably, people ask mental health professionals for some tips on living: "Hey Doc, do you have any suggestions on how I can...?"

While the Ten Commandments and the Golden Rule are certainly key principles to follow, try adding these to your list:

• You have good qualities — focus on *them*. Many people who come for psychotherapy enter treatment with complaints about their negative traits; they seem to forget anything positive about themselves.

So, if it's a generous nature, loyalty, a friendly smile or the ability to keep a secret, keep your positive traits out front.

• Whatever you do, don't rate your *self*. Rate instead your traits, performances, abilities and skills. Remember that being a good student doesn't mean you are a good person any more than being a poor tennis player means you are a worthless person. Keep your overall worth outside of your individual skills.

• Learn to look at your problems honestly. Facing your problems may seem to be the very thing you most want to avoid, but find someone you like and trust to *share* the burden with.

• Instead of focusing on what you get from other people, focus on what others get from contact with you. Do they hear nothing but your complaints, stresses, and problems? Or do they receive something that may be helpful, refreshing, or even inspirational? When your focus is on doing and giving rather than receiving and getting, you are more likely to have something returned to you. It has been said that if you want something from another person, give it away first. That is a great rule of thumb to keep in mind in day-to-day interactions with others, especially in close relationships.

Look for positive qualities in yourself and *in others*. While this may sound trite, still it is important for healthy mental functioning.

It is certainly easy to find faults with other people and yourself. The person who truly lives in a healthy and happy way appears to be the one who excels in finding the good points in others. When you stop and think about the truly charismatic, magnetic, friendly people you know — those who appear to attract people wherever they go — I believe you'll find this particular trait.

• One of the most difficult tasks in dealing with other people is accepting them as they are. It's terribly important to avoid controlling someone else and thereby implying that you are not satisfied with who they are.

One couple whom I have treated in marital counseling comes to mind. He was quite unaccepting of a particular habit of hers — he demanded, demanded, and demanded even more that she be different. Of course this only resulted in her becoming more and more defensive and, in a rather passive-aggressive way, avoiding changing because it was her one way — her one weapon — of gaining control over him.

Couples who are "into" controlling each other, power plays, and winning each interaction, have a relationship that is likely doomed to fail. Look around and you will see that those relationships that appear to be the strongest are comprised of two independent adults who accept each other's traits and habits, good and bad. So bear with your partner — and remember that that person must put up with you as well.

• Let's talk about success and failure. Everyone has failures and everyone has successes — no matter how big or how small. Failures are not something to worry over, they are something to learn from, take from, and grow from. Try to remember your successes and don't spend too much time worrying about the failures.

• Many times when I do group psychotherapy, I find that one of the most important healing aspects of the treatment is something called "universality." That is, coming to an awareness of the fact that you are not the only one in the world who has problems and, quite likely, your problems are no better or worse than anyone else's. How many of you would, in fact, truly trade problems with anyone else? Everyone is occasionally worried or discouraged, including you. It's important to *accept* that fact, and keep going.

I have been carrying a poem with me since the end of my freshman year in college. The poem is called simply, "Don't Quit." I wish I could tell you who wrote it, but I do not know. It was given to me with "Anon." at the bottom. (I also wish that I could tell you that I wrote it, but I did not!) It's worth taking a moment to share it with you.

When things go wrong, as they sometimes will,
When the road you are trudging seems all uphill,
When the funds are low and the debts are high,
And you want to smile, but have to sigh,
When care is pressing you down a bit — rest if
*   you must,*
But don't you quit.

Life is queer with its twists and its turns,
As every one of us sometimes learns,
And many a fellow turns about
When he might have won had he stuck it out.
Don't give up though the pace seems slow — you may
*   succeed with another blow.*

Often the goal is nearer than it seems
To a faint and faltering man;
Often the struggler has given up
When he might have captured the victor's cup;
And he learned too late when the night came down
How close he was to the golden crown.

Success is failure turned inside out — the silver
  tint of the clouds of doubt,
And you never can tell how close you are,
It may be near when it seems afar;
So stick to the fight when you're hardest hit —
It's when things seem worse that you mustn't quit.

Of course, it's important to note here that sticking with a bad situation (a dead-end job, or unhealthy relationship) just to avoid being a "quitter" does not insure success. One must also know when to bow out gracefully.

• Be careful not to over-extend yourself terms of promises and responsibilities. Learn how to say no. Promise to do only those things that, in fact, you fully intend to do and are able to do. By doing this, you will avoid disappointing yourself and others.

• Finally, remember that people, not things, are most important in your life. I have never heard a dying man cry out for his shiny new Mercedes, his brand new Palm Springs condo, or his large-screen television. People do cry out for other people. Keep a human perspective on life.

Perhaps you have heard many of these thoughts before. They bear repeating here, to encourage you to *think* about where you are — and where you are going.

Don't Should on Yourself

At its best, guilt keeps us from killing each other. At its worst, it allows us to kill ourselves. In the right amount and at the right time, it serves as a reminder that we have done — or are about to do — something wrong. This article is not about what's right with guilt. It's about what's wrong with it and how to overcome it, if it's overcome you.

- "I don't deserve such success."
- "I shouldn't feel such happiness."
- "I shouldn't put myself first."
- "I should have behaved differently."
- "I should have told him I loved him more often."

These and many other similar statements are the early seeds for overwhelming guilt. Who hasn't "should" on themselves to the point of feeling crippled by the fear and anxiety aroused by guilt? These worries, in turn, may bring on a whole spectrum of emotional ills, from chronic fatigue to other self-punishing states, such as sexual frigidity, drug and alcohol addiction, depression, and suicide. Far too many people self-destruct promising careers or relationships due to full-blown, needless guilt. It keeps you from doing what you enjoy and can often keep you a slave to someone else.

Perhaps you can recall a "martyr mother" example from your own childhood, who paralyzed — and enraged — you by a guilt-inducing statement such as, "You go out if you must...I'll be (sigh) O.K."

Children who are severely riddled with guilt, or unjustly accused of wrong-doing may go in one of a couple of directions. They may be so incapable of living with the guilt that's been drilled into them that they rebel with drugs, antisocial behavior or the like. Or they give in to the guilt and grow up believing they *are* totally worthless, rotten, and undeserving. Extreme feelings of guilt can make some folks believe life is so unbearable that suicide is the only way out.

Some accident-prone patients I've treated have revealed in psychotherapy that they are basically guilt-ridden; they alleviate the feeling by literally punishing themselves through their accidents.

Most people can handle their guilt feelings, but sometimes the guilt is pushed far beneath the surface — out of conscious awareness. Such persons require professional help to bring the feelings back to light and to assist the person in learning to cope more effectively.

To help rid yourself of unwanted guilt, *stop "shoulding" on yourself.* Most feelings of guilt or shame stem from *demanding* that one do *exactly* the right thing by others, *always* putting others before yourself. Renowned psychologist Dr. Albert Ellis, says, "Although you had better *not* needlessly harm others or commit antisocial acts, you can make yourself feel sorry and irresponsible if and when you do, but need not totally damn yourself as a human and thus sorely afflict yourself with self-damaging shame and guilt."

Basically, experts agree that you would do well to learn the difference between reasonable and unreasonable expectations of yourself. Re-examine the rules prescribed by parents, friends, and society. Keep what's sound and sensible, and dump the unwarranted and foolish.

Ellis points out that the three major "musts'" or "shoulds" that disturb most people are: 1) "I *should* perform well and be loved by everyone"; 2) "Other people *should* treat me fairly and kindly"; and 3) "Conditions *should* be favorable and easy!"

You can't possibly always be patient and even-tempered towards those you love. Stop tormenting yourself if you're not. Your responsibilities towards your aging parents may be far less than you've irrationally imposed on yourself. Do what's right for you — without injuring anyone else or acting irresponsibly. Give up the idea of perfection. Use the phrase, "it would be better" instead of "should," or "have to," or "ought," or "must."

Finally, if you have goofed, accept it, learn from it and go on. You can feel *sorry*, without stunting yourself with guilt. Downing yourself (which is, according to Dr. Ellis, a major part of guilt) is never likely to help — no matter what you've done.

The "Other PMS"

If you are looking for information on Pre-Menstrual Syndrome (PMS), you are in the wrong place. This article is about Mantell's version of PMS: *Personalizing, Magnifying* and *Shoulding.* Not quite Pre-Menstrual Syndrome, but the results are perhaps even more overwhelming. This version of PMS is experienced by men and children as well as women. And it doesn't occur for just two weeks per month. This version can, and often does, occur daily. For some of you, it may even be a steady way of life.

Let me describe this syndrome to you and see if you identify with any of the symptoms. First, let's look at *Personalizing.*

You call a friend with whom you haven't spoken for quite a while. She says she'd love to talk to you but can't just now because another friend of hers is on the "other line" (call waiting, of course). You immediately decide this friend is angry at you. After all, if she weren't, wouldn't she drop the other caller and devote time to you?

Another example. You have been volunteering your time and energy to a charity. Each week you donate your efforts for one project or another. When it comes time to select individuals for a special committee, you are not selected.

You instantly assume it must be that the people who made the selection do not like you.

Personalizing is a way of thinking that shows you believe others are focused on you. It rests on the assumption that if something bad (or good) happens, it is your responsibility. Even if you had nothing to do with it.

You may often feel guilt or responsibility, or find yourself apologizing a great deal. You assume ownership of other people's problems. In the extreme, you may find yourself becoming very suspicious of others. You may "read other people's minds" and assume they are thinking ill of you. Or likewise a smile on the face of someone passing you at work *must* mean he or she "is interested" in you.

Magnifying. Ever look at life through a magnifying glass? Small pebbles look like boulders. And boulders look like Mt. Everest. And Mt. Everest looks like...

Small problems become big problems. And big problems become insurmountable. But they really are not. Under the magnifying glass, they just look that way.

You may always feel you are under enormous pressures. You may find that your life is filled *only* with major problems. One grey hair means it's time for a wig. Getting a "B" on a test means ultimate failure. Being rejected by one potential employer means no one will ever hire you. And one small success means total, complete, irreversible success.

Shoulding. This is one of my favorites. He should do this. She should do that. They shouldn't go here. We shouldn't "should" on ourselves so much. Ugh! With all of this shoulding going on, things are getting pretty smelly.

No one can ever live up to all of the things one "should" do. If you have this absolutistic demanding approach to yourself or others, life will inevitably get you down.

You will feel disappointment in yourself and in others. You will feel frustration, resentment and anger. You will certainly find little satisfaction as you see people unable or unwilling to comply with your "shoulding" demands.

"But I'm not demanding that you stay home, I'm just

saying you shouldn't go out," said one father to his furious young adult daughter.

Sure it sounds funny. It isn't though. It's really kind of sad, isn't it? When you tell someone else what they *should* (must, ought to, have to) do, you are demanding they be different than they are. What right do you have to do that to another adult human? None.

You may suggest, "I think it would be better if you did this or that." But demanding one "should" is a set up for negative feelings.

The other person who chooses to comply with your order may feel resentful toward you. The person who chooses not to comply (and it's always their choice) may feel guilt in relationship to you. Who needs these sorts of complicated ties?

To suggest what *you think* is better or wiser recognizes the integrity of the other adult's choice. That is an acknowledgement of equality in a relationship.

So this is Mantell's version of PMS. Personalizing, Magnifying and Shoulding. If you feel depressed, anxious or hostile, look for one (or all) of these thinking patterns. You are sure to find them.

These thinking distortions are the basis of a great deal of human misery. They are the obstacles I most frequently find people putting in their own way.

The next time you feel one of the feelings I just listed — depression, anxiety or hostility — stop for a moment. Walk away from the situation. Make a mental diagram of three columns headed "P," "M," or "S." List each of your particular thoughts in the column in which it fits. Make a mental note of how you are personalizing, magnifying, or shoulding.

You will find it easy then to erase the non-productive thought(s) and substitute something more realistic and rational. Your feelings will change to more normal, less overwhelmingly negative ones. And your PMS will come under your control. It won't solve all of your problems, but I can assure you if this sort of PMS is one of your frustrations, taking better control of it will enable you to tackle life's other problems in a calmer, clearer and healthier way.

Are You in Control?

At one time or another nearly everyone has felt as though they are losing control. And who among us hasn't complained of feeling controlled by everyone and everything?

Some believe that the feeling of self-control, of determining what happens to you in your life, has far-reaching consequences for all areas of life, including physical and mental well-being.

People who are in control of themselves generally have a positive mental attitude and a healthier outlook on life than those who feel victimized by others. In an interesting recent study done in a nursing home, for example, residents were allowed to decide what they could eat, when the phone in their rooms could ring, and how the furniture in their rooms should be arranged. While this is not a great deal of control over one's life, if you have spent any time in a nursing home recently, you will know that this is a lot more control than many residents often have. Guess what happened? The elderly men and women residents described themselves as being happier and more alert. Most importantly, there was a lower mortality rate over a period of eighteen months — by fifty percent! So having a say over what happens in one's life affects not only the quality of one's life but the quantity as well.

Those who have a great need to be in control have typically achieved well in school, have opinions that are not easily swayed and — in a finding that should make Dr. Ruth happy — have more frequent sex and greater use of contraceptives. Isn't that interesting? Professor Jerry Burger at the University of Santa Clara told me, "People who are high in the need for control report having more different kinds of sexual experience and sex more frequently than those with lower needs for control." He went on to say, "The highs use more reliable methods of contraception such as pills and diaphragms than did the lows, who used withdrawal, douching and guessing, or nothing at all. This reflects the need to be responsible for what they do."

On the downside, those who need to be in control all the time also tend to be more susceptible to depression when they feel they're not in control.

Back to the nursing homes for a moment. The effect of hopelessness and helplessness grows with age, which is one reason older people are often adversely affected when they *have to* move. When the elderly are forced to move (and therefore have less control over their lives) we see increases in hospitalizations, nursing home admissions, strokes, and chest pain from heart disease. One researcher at Yale University, Judith Rodin, has found "evidence of stronger effects of uncontrollable stress on the immune system of elderly people." She believes that the fragility of the elderly increases their susceptibility to frustrations that come from loss of control. In a related laboratory experiment, Dr. Rodin found diminished functioning of immune systems in lab animals that had no control over the severity or duration of electric shocks given to them. When the animals in her study were able to end the shocks, there were no adverse effects on the immune system — even though both groups had the same total amount of shock. Once again, *control* of their situation was the key factor.

Another fascinating study involves control in the work place. Two groups of people were separated into large work rooms, with clerical workers in each group. Both groups had "bad noise" pumped into their music system. One group was told that they had a button that they could control and could turn down the noise if they so desired. The other group was not given that instruction. The group without the button showed higher instances in absenteeism, headaches, other aches and pains, and "stress." The group with the button showed no signs of stress and fewer physical symptoms. How many times did the group with the button actually turn down the noise? If you guessed none, you were right. Fascinating isn't it? Just the mere fact that they knew they *could* control the noise was enough, even though they actually did not.

In another study on control, two groups were divided on a variable psychologists call the "Type A — Type B Personality." Type A's have what is called the hurry-up illness. They are highly competitive, aggressive, angry much of the time and translate their life into numbers. They always need to be first in line — although they may wait just as long as if they were last. Type B's are much more mellow, calm, and relaxed.

In this study by Suzanne Miller of Temple University, Type A's were told that their partners (Type B's) had faster reaction times. The Type A's were told that one of the pair should push a button in order to save both of them from electric shock. Guess who did it? The Type A's. Even though they knew that their partners may have had faster reaction times, the Type A's preferred to have the responsibility. In fact, the Type B's did not have a faster reaction time, the Type A's were merely under that impression. Type A people tend to make more and more desperate attempts to exert control, even when faced with uncontrollable situations.

Some researchers believe that repeated and frustrated attempts for control can lead to increases in the level of blood substances that studies have found are linked to atherosclerosis.

And what about the work place? Well, one study that followed people for three years found that workers who had dictatorial bosses (those who set down the rules for how work was to be carried out) had a general resentment and distrust towards the entire company. Those whose bosses gave them more leeway in their work expressed more trust in the company and were more satisfied with their work.

The same thing occurs with teachers and students. Generally speaking, when teachers are more controlling in a classroom, their students forget more of what they learned than do students whose teachers allow more autonomy. This was shown in an interesting study by Richard Ryan and Wendy Grolnick, who summarize by saying "force-feeding facts may lead to higher test scores but the more the student feels control from the outside, the less pleasure he feels from inside. He ends up being turned off to learning."

What does all this have to do with you? I advocate that you look for areas in your life in which you think you do not have control. Evaluate whether you in fact *are* out of control and, if so, begin to do something about that. One easy thing to do is to change your "have to's" to "choose to's." That is to say, ask yourself what you "have to" do. Then, instead of saying, "I have to _____," say, "I choose to _____." I believe you will find that many of the things you believe you "have to" do are actually things, when you come down to it, you "choose to" do. There is little need to live your life as a victim and — as you can see from the research I've summarized above — there are many rewards from living your life in a more self-controlled manner.

Want to Impress Someone?

A friend is a person who knows you...and still likes you. But if you are one of those people who won't let anyone get to know the "real you," the emotional price you may be paying could be a great deal higher than you realize.

Some have referred to this as the "Social Chameleon" syndrome. Who doesn't want to make a positive impression on others? Most successful people are concerned with what impact they have on others and attempt to make a good impression on friends, co-workers, family members or business associates.

But what about the social chameleons who make it a way of life — who are always striving to make the best impression they can? Well, recent research says they are doing so at a high price.

Dr. Mark Snyder, a social psychologist at the University of Minnesota, and the key researcher in this area, said that people who always must be the "right person in the right place at the right time," have become especially sensitive to the ways others react to them. He calls these ever-changing personality types "high self-monitors."

His research uncovered these traits:

1. They carefully scrutinize others so they know how to react based on what they believe others expect.

2. They strive to be accepted, liked and approved of by behaving as others expect.

3. With different people, they will act very differently, so as to mold themselves to what others want.

4. Social chameleons thrive on changing their image to always please others. They are especially comfortable with inconsistency.

So, if you are one of these high self-monitors, what else has research discovered about you? Well, for one thing, paradoxically, you probably have less stable intimate relationships. And what's more, you are likely to prefer a wide range of friends, with different friends for different activities.

In counseling men and women who discover this style in themselves, I am often struck by how empty many feel. ''I don't know who *I* am, anymore. I'm always trying to get someone else's approval, so I act like them and forget what I really think. Sometimes I wonder if I really exist anymore. I feel like a mirror for everyone else.'' These are common thoughts for social chameleons who are willing to look inside of themselves with someone they trust.

Why is it so important to gain approval from others that they lose themselves in the process? Some have such a fragile sense of themselves, believe themselves to be so bad, that their own approval isn't worth very much, so they must have it from others.

This is, of course, a set-up for depression when others do not give the approval they need. In the extreme examples are con artists who will say or do whatever is necessary to get what they want. In a sense, some folks are so empty that they are ''approval con artists.'' They don't want your money, they want you to like them.

These actors, acting ''as-if'' they are like you when they are with you — and acting ''as-if'' they are like someone else when they are with them — are sad shells of people. Sad, because somewhere they have come to believe that they are not OK and others are.

While anyone who is a successful salesperson, politician, actor, or diplomat uses these skills frequently in real life, it must be seen that these are only skills at best.

When making the best possible impression becomes a way of life, when it becomes an addiction, when you panic about the real you getting out, it's time to get some help — without trying to impress the therapist.

Is Anger a Four-Letter Word?

O.K., you get angry once in awhile. So who doesn't? People who tell me, "I never fight with my wife," or "I *never* get angry," lead me to be more than a bit suspicious.

Why? Because *everyone* gets angry at some time or another. Some people have learned such self-control that they won't *show* their feelings. But their doctors know they're angry. It shows in migraine headaches, hypertension, ulcers, skin problems, even sexual problems and allergies. I'm not suggesting these problems are always or even *most* always related to angry feelings, but there *is* a relationship between feelings and physical well-being.

King Solomon (Proverbs 17:22) said, "A merry heart doeth good like a medicine; but a broken spirit drieth the bones."

Norman Cousins, in his book, *The Healing Heart,* noted that "the medical literature was replete with data showing that panic, fear, frustration, and depression all levied a fearsome toll on human physiology... inviting illness or intensifying it." The positive emotions, according to Cousins, serve as a "bullet-proof vest that protects us against the effects of emotional assaults."

Anger, as an amalgamation of many negative feelings, can and should be expressed — in a constructive, healthy way. I believe that people who know how to express anger in an appropriately assertive — not aggressive — way, are quite fortunate.

But it is a skill that can be taught and learned in relatively easy, practical and straightforward ways. In counseling children who fight, husbands and wives who bicker and argue — men and women who feel abused and taken advantage of a great deal of the time — one thing is clear. They *all* need to become more *assertive*. They need to prevent the build-up of hostile feelings by utilizing better ways of expressing anger. So, what *is* assertive behavior?

It's defined by psychologists Robert E. Alberti, Ph.D. and Michael L. Emmons, Ph.D., in their pioneering assertiveness book, *Your Perfect Right,* as "behavior which promotes equality in human relationships, enabling us to act in our own best interests, to stand up for ourselves without undue anxiety, to express feelings honestly and comfortably, to exercise personal rights without denying the rights of others." Being assertive, letting others know what you feel in a way that doesn't put anyone else down, may often result in getting what you want.

Then again, it may not.

Aggressive behavior is always at the expense of someone else. You'll get your way, but you'll step on someone else to do it.

Non-assertive behavior is usually self-denying, non-expressive, usually results in not getting what you want, and allows others to choose and decide for you.

Here's an example from everyday life: You've been looking forward to trying a new restaurant and finally have your chance. Everything is going great until the steak you ordered rare — the $15 steak — is delivered quite well-done by the smiling waiter, with his gracious, "Enjoy!"

What do you do?

...swallow hard, sharpen your knife and saw into the cordovan-like meat, muttering all the time, thinking you need shoe polish instead of steak sauce?

...beckon "grinning gourmet," call him the "stupidest, most incompetent nerd you've ever run across" for insulting you with the over-cooked steak, *demand* he immediately bring you another — and in the process ruin everyone's evening?

...motion to the waiter, say simply, "I ordered a rare steak; this is well-done; please bring me another, this time rare"?

In the third (assertive) style, no one is put down, you stand up for your rights and everyone leaves satisfied, treated fairly, and the waiter may even get a proper tip.

Being assertive is easier once you learn how. Of course it takes practice. So practice — without hurting anyone — yourself included. Common situations that provide great opportunities for practice include returning faulty merchandise to a store; asking a neighbor to quiet down; starting a conversation with a stranger; public speaking; asking for a favor.

Couples often find themselves attacking each other instead of the problem confronting them. One has to be right, or the "winner." As in any sport, such as tennis, if you *always* win, eventually it gets boring — and you find fewer and fewer people to play with. In life, if you must always have your way at the expense of someone else, your bones may not dry up, but your relationships surely will.

Playing the "nice guy" is stressful because that role requires us to deny significant emotional parts of ourselves — we must pretend that a portion of our reality is not there. The solution is to break away from the nice guy role and work hard at being more honest with ourselves and others.

If practicing assertiveness doesn't help you express anger more spontaneously and appropriately, you may be harboring feelings that need professional attention.

Norman Cousins, in the summary of his book, wrote that "confidence, deep purpose, joyousness, laughter, and the will to live are good conditioning agents and their value should never be underestimated." There is no need to spend of your life being angry. If you can't get beyond hurting others, or feeling hurt yourself much of the time, reach out for help.

ⒹDefensiveness

A mistake is a lesson on its way to being learned. At least that's how I look at it. So why get defensive when you commit a faux pas? Or worse yet, why get defensive when you haven't made a mistake?

I've always believed that when you buy trouble, there's never a rebate. So listen in on this couple, and see if it sounds familiar.

He: You're so upset. What's wrong?

She: Oh, like you really care to know.

He: Sure I do, otherwise I wouldn't have asked.

She: Oh, you'll think it's dumb.

He: Try me. I will not think it's dumb.

She: I missed ''Dynasty'' this week, O.K.? See, I told you it was stupid.

He: Why do you always assume that I will think you're dumb or stupid? I don't!

She: Well, you don't get upset like I do. Maybe I am too defensive, but I always think you are going to think you're smarter than me.

Do you hear the defensiveness? It is a common emotional reaction in people. When you feel defensive about something, large or small, you are not fully in control of yourself. You are reacting based on some irrational notion that you must protect yourself from harm. In this case, the harm you protect yourself from is anticipated psycho-social harm. Not physical harm, but social trauma. She won't like you, he'll think you're stupid, they won't respect you, or he will make fun of you.

If you identify your fear early, defensiveness can be minimized, if not averted altogether. Defensiveness on the job, in social interaction, in school, or in a relationship is a potentially damaging emotion since it usually blocks free communication: it inhibits the free expression of primary feelings such as hurt, fear, and frustration. You believe you have to act in a certain way to keep the other person from really seeing or knowing what you are feeling. Yet this communication is the very thing which would help in the situation. Truly effective, interpersonally secure individuals *express* hurt or fear, instead of behaving defensively.

What can you do to identify when you are acting defensively? First, whenever you become sarcastic, resentful or angry, defensiveness *may* be the culprit. Not always, but look for it as a possibility.

How else do you protect yourself from the onslaughts of others? Accusations and name-calling are other indicators of defensiveness. The best defense is *not* a good offense. It is the free expression of honest feelings.

Blaming or finding fault with others can be a sign that self-protection is actually what you are feeling. Assuming that you have been accused of something is yet another sure-fire sign of defensive behavior.

All this leads to misinterpreting others' behavior and motives, and to potentially destructive conflict.

The key is to understand that you set up your own "boogey man," act as if the imagined harm is real and *actually* hurtful, and then hide behind defensiveness of one sort or another.

Hey, c'mon. Stop scaring yourself so much. You create your monsters and defend yourself against them just as if the threat were genuine. Sound irrational? You bet it is. But it is a great deal healthier in the long run to be able to live life non-defensively. So he thinks he's smarter. So she thinks she's prettier. Is it worth twisting yourself up in a psychological and physical knot over it? Like the headline I saw the other day, "Impotence is on the rise." It just doesn't make any sense.

Life's Stop Signs

Picture this. You are driving on the freeways on your way to work. The roads are crowded. "Too crowded," you say to yourself. And then it happens. In the midst of morning rush-hour bumper-to-bumper traffic, an accident occurs. Nothing too serious, just enough to bring traffic to a complete standstill.

You look to your left and you see a driver turning all shades of red, purple and blue with anger and frustration. She pounds two fists on the dashboard and appears to be muttering and shouting a string of obscenities — as if that could help the traffic jam.

You look to your right and see a different picture. There, in the middle of the freeway standstill, in rush-hour traffic, is someone who is reclining, with a half-smile on his face, seeming to be enjoying the beat of the music on the radio. Or maybe enjoying a daydream of a positive experience, a beautiful place, a favorite person, or some other relaxing scene — as if that will help the flow of traffic.

You then look in your rear view mirror and see... yourself. How do *you* respond to life's inevitable bumps on the road, accidents, scratches on your new car, or red lights when you're in a hurry?

For those of you who are what psychologists and physicians refer to as "Type A" personalities, you probably feel your blood pressure rising just *thinking* of such a scene. Type A behavior includes the following:

- competitive — at work, home and play
- feels chronic time urgency
- is very impatient when waiting for other people
- walks, eats and works rapidly
- feels important when busy
- feels guilty when relaxing
- seldom stops to relax alone or enjoy life's beauty.

On the other hand, if you are a "Type B" personality, you probably are more understanding about such things as traffic jams and may even use them to your advantage as a time to relax.

Type B behavior includes:
- no time urgency
- ability to leave a task incomplete without feeling anxious or frustrated
- patience with other people
- play without competition
- relaxation without guilt
- enjoyment of *being* and not just doing
- taking time to appreciate the beautiful, and the simple pleasures of life.

Meyer Friedman, M.D., and Ray Rosenman, M.D., who wrote the book, *Type A Behavior and Your Heart* in 1974, found that Type A behavior types were several times more likely to develop heart disease than other people.

Of course, there are times when Type A behavior is called for and times when Type B behavior is appropriate. To manage stress effectively you have to know the difference and know how to turn each on — and off.

Life is filled with what I refer to as "positive stop signs." Not just the red stop signs we see at traffic intersections, but long lines at the bank or supermarket, waiting for the computer to authorize your credit card, waiting for late airplanes, the concert to begin, or your dinner to arrive. These instances and more like them are life's way of giving you a chance to slow down.

But how do many people, especially Type A's, react to these positive stop signs? By believing instead that "life is out to get me," or "life is sticking it to me again." Nonsense. What a wasteful way to look at a chance to take a deep breath and relax. Does pounding the dash, blowing steam from your nose, screaming and demanding do anything to hurry things up? Of course not.

But wait. It does do something.

Go back to the rush-hour traffic and look at the man blowing up again. While he isn't doing anything to help the flow of traffic to improve, he is doing something. He is, quite simply, killing himself. Or making others he is with most miserable. But he surely is not helping himself or the problem with which he is confronted.

Begin looking at positive stop signs as opportunities to slow down your frenetic pace. If you can do something to help the situation along, go ahead and do it. If not, recognize it and enjoy the chance to just sit back and pause — even if it is for only a moment.

Herbert Benson, M.D., the Harvard Medical School cardiologist noted in his book, *The Relaxation Response*, that all methods of relaxation have much in common. Here's a simple way to do it:

1. Sit quietly in a comfortable position.

2. Close your eyes.

3. Beginning at your feet and progressing up to your face, deeply relax all your muscles. Keep them relaxed.

4. Breathe through your nose. Become aware of your breathing. As you breathe out, say the word *one* silently to yourself. Continue the pattern: breathe in...out, "one"; in...out, "one"; and so on. Breathe easily and naturally.

5. Continue for 10 to 20 minutes. You may open your eyes to check the time, but do not use an alarm. When you finish, sit quietly for several minutes, first with your eyes closed and later with your eyes opened. Do not stand up for a few minutes.

6. Do not worry about whether you are successful in achieving a deep level of relaxation. Maintain a passive attitude and permit relaxation to occur at its own pace. When distracting thoughts occur, try to ignore them by not dwelling on them and return to repeating "one." With practice, the response should come with little effort. Practice the technique once or twice daily, but not within two hours after any meal,

since the digestive processes seem to inhibit the relaxation response.

If you practice the relaxation response regularly, you are more likely to come to see life's "stop signs" as opportunities rather than enemies. You may, over time, help yourself move from the Type A position toward the Type B position. And at the very least, you'll be able to handle our ever-growing traffic jams better.

It's Not Too Late to Change the Way You Live

Which of the following statements can you agree with?
- I don't make enough money to do what I want.
- I regret my mistakes in raising my children.
- It's too late to make any changes in my career.
- My personality is pretty well set.
- I try to be satisfied with what I have and not think so much about the things I probably won't get.
- Life doesn't change much from year to year.
- My parents are the cause of many of my problems.
- My greatest concern is my health.

If you find yourself agreeing with most of these statements, and life's hassles seem to be getting to you, don't despair. There is much you can do to change the way you are living your life.

If you are experiencing a mid-life transition and are in the 35-50 year age bracket, your health and life-style may be of special concern for you. If you are younger and are concerned about your *future* health, this is a good time to check on your priorities. Let's take a look at the "good life" you have been leading and see what you can do about it. Why? Because it may just be killing you.

First of all, recognize that most people to some extent, choose the way in which they will die. How you live, moment by moment, may be responsible for determining what will kill you and when. The saying, "Eat, drink, and die young," is worth thinking about for a moment.

The big killers in our society today aren't germs anymore. These can be controlled by a host of antibiotics which give physicians control over bacteria. No, the big killers today seem to be related to living habits. You could be making yourself the potential victim of heart disease or a stroke — from an all-too-typical American diet rich in fat and cholesterol, from high blood pressure, from cigarette smoking, or from obesity. Or, you could be enhancing your potential for being a victim of cancer, cirrhosis of the liver, emphysema, or bronchitis.

The trends start early in life. Unfortunately there are no vaccines which can prevent such threats to life. Cleaning up your life-style is the best cure — and the best prevention.

The U.S. Department of Health, and Human Services, in its "Forward Plan for Health," noted that, "It has become clear only by *preventing* disease, rather than treating it later, can we hope to achieve any major improvement in the nation's health."

Four reasons often cited by health experts help explain how bad health habits have crept up on us without a great deal of early warning. The first has to do with the sense of *time urgency* — young children (who are at the prime of their lives and feeling good) don't care about the risks which are associated with the dangers of future disease. It can often take ten to thirty years of abuse with cigarettes and fatty diets to produce lung cancer or heart disease. *The illusion of immortality* — that it will happen to someone else — is also tough to combat.

Next, simply turn on your television set, open a magazine or newspaper, and you will find advertising for many potentially *dangerous products,* including cigarettes and alcohol. These are subliminally equated with a life-style of "fun." Finally, while many physicians find their time taken up with healing the sick and injured, it's only recently that the medical profession has begun paying serious attention to *preventive medicine.*

So, is your life-style bad for your health?

Two physicians, Dr. Lewis Robbins and Dr. Jack Hall of the Methodist Hospital in Indianapolis, developed a "Life-Style Risk Analysis Questionnaire" which is being used by the Canadian government in a campaign to improve living habits. They focused on the following key factors in assessing a healthy life-style: smoking; alcohol; trimness; physical activity; the use of prescription drugs; the use of non-prescription drugs (other than alcohol and tobacco); seatbelt use; tranquility; mixing driving with alcohol or other drugs; water safety; blood cholesterol, glucose and blood pressure checks; and, for women only, the use of drugs during pregnancy, breast examinations, and pap smears.

These are, in part, the very same characteristics which University of Pennsylvania biologist, Dr. Ingrid Waldron, was quoted as saying are related to why men have a 60 percent higher early death rate than women. In one interview she stated, "The behaviors expected of males in our society seem to make a major contribution to their elevated mortality." Certainly, as more women enter high-stress professions, the traditionally male life-style — high-fat diet, cigarette smoking, job stress, little exercise — is being labeled as the culprit in the rise in women's heart attacks and mortality as well.

What can you do about it if you find yourself being described here? Dr. Lester Breslow, the Dean of the School of Public Health at UCLA, has found seven habits which he believes are associated with a longer life span: (1) eat three meals at regular times each day instead of snacking; (2) eat breakfast every day; (3) exercise; (4) sleep seven or eight hours at night; (5) do not smoke; (6) maintain moderate weight; and (7) do not consume more than a moderate amount of alcohol (three ounces daily). Breslow concluded that by switching from an unhealthy life-style to a healthier one, an individual can figure on adding about fourteen years to his or her life!

The United States Department of Health and Human Services suggests that by avoiding cigarettes, following sensible drinking habits, using care in taking prescription drugs, eating sensibly (throwing away the salt shaker, getting down to your ideal weight, eliminating saturated fats, and eating more fruits, vegetables and other foods containing fiber), exercising regularly, handling stress properly, and being safety-conscious, you can go a long way in improving an otherwise potentially dangerous life-style.

Laurence Morehouse and Leonard Gross, co-authors of the book, *Total Fitness,* noted that an individual who has been avoiding exercise, and then begins an aerobic exercise training program, can go to about 80 percent of his or her conditioning level in just one month. Dr. Kenneth Cooper, who authored the book, *Total Well-Being,* summarized research indicating that after only three months of aerobic conditioning the heart rates of middle-aged men plunged from 72 beats per minute to 55 beats per minute. This indicates a strengthening of the heart muscle, enabling it to beat fewer times while pumping a greater volume of blood. This is more typical of conditioned athletes. Cooper found lung capacity increased with aerobic training as well.

The research, then, is clear. Physical deterioration that begins at age thirty can lead to a 50 percent reduction in most body functions by age seventy. But regular exercise can delay this process for as much as twenty years.

What is regular aerobic exercise? A minimum of three sessions per week, every other day, thirty minutes in duration of continuous activity — running, jogging, swimming, jumping rope, walking, dancing, or biking. Make it intense enough to perspire, increase your heart rate and breathe deeply. Give yourself a cool-down period of at least fifteen minutes before jumping into a shower.

Eating on the run, when you're not hungry, or while you're talking about or thinking about unpleasant topics, are all poor habits and ought to be avoided. Sugar, caffeine, nicotine, alcohol, white flour, and red meat? Only in moderation. They can be among the more detrimental nutritional stressors. There are "anti-stress foods": bananas, almonds, raisins, broccoli, spinach, wheat germ, sunflower seeds and honey. These are especially recommended for the high-stress person and best fulfill your nervous system needs.

The *emotional* payoffs of regular exercise, proper nutrition, proper sleep and relaxation are difficult to quantify. But ask anyone who follows that sort of a plan. They feel better, feel more energetic, and generally cope with life's hassles quite well. They have an outlet to burn off the body's stress chemicals. The euphoric feeling some runners and those who are involved in vigorous exercise describe, comes from the body's natural production of opiate-like hormones called "beta-endorphins." These are natural tranquilizers that are involved in lowering blood pressure and curbing appetite. Their effects last for up to an hour or more. Running may be an effective aid in the treatment of some forms of depression because of the production of these natural anti-stress chemicals.

So you have a choice. You can go on killing yourself, stressing yourself, doing little to help yourself. Or you can change your life-style habits, begin proper aerobic exercise, relaxation, nutrition and sleep patterns, and go a long way in protecting yourself from the ill-effects of stress. Check with your physician and/or exercise specialist for guidance about what's proper for you before beginning any exercise or nutrition program.

Part 2.

Your Relationships

They begin before conception and they extend beyond death. In between, it's struggle, struggle, struggle. Once we learn how to deal with ourselves, and often before we learn to deal with ourselves, we have to learn to deal with each other.

An elderly gentleman once confided to me his formula for a long-lasting relationship: "I go my way. She goes her way. And every now and then we meet in the bedroom." Of course, it's not always that easy.

Every day each of us confronts a complex tangle of relationships, some equal, some subordinate or dominating, some casual, some intimate. We must greet lover, children, parents, friends, fellow workers, bosses, employees, clients, in-laws, outlaws and the butcher, the baker and the candlestick maker. No wonder we're tired at the end of the day.

How do we relate to all this? Sometimes we don't. The issues before us can be significant. How do you deal with a loved one's death, or face someone you love who's dying? How do you rekindle a failing marriage?

After distributing an examination on medieval history, a college professor once remarked to his class, "You'll note 'hat the questions I have posed for you this afternoon are really quite simple." Then he paused and his features twisted into a sinister smile. "The answers," he said, "are a little more difficult."

The following section presents relationships that may be familiar to you. Coping successfully with those relationships, and your feelings about them, is what it's all about.

Friends Can Be Good Medicine

Ask anyone. Smoking, over-drinking, poor nutrition, lack of exercise — these can all have ill effects on our health. What many people don't recognize is that our relationships — or lack of them — can affect our health as well. Supportive personal relationships, in fact, can help protect both mental and physical well-being.

Here are some facts from the "Friends Can Be Good Medicine" project, sponsored by the California Department of Mental Health:

• Rates of mental hospitalization are approximately *5-10 times greater* for separated, divorced and widowed adults as for married people.

• Socially isolated persons have *2-3 times* the overall risk of *dying prematurely* as do people who maintain supportive relationships.

• Pregnant women under stress without supportive relationships have *3 times* the number of *complications* as do women with supportive relationships.

• Among men who are fired from work, those who have close personal supports have fewer psychological or health problems than those with less social support.

• Terminal cancer has a higher incidence among divorced individuals of both sexes than among those who are married.

• Women who have a confidant are less likely to become seriously depressed.

The Department of Mental Health's report indicates that all of the research isn't in yet. Nobody knows exactly how our friendships work to protect our health. It may be that those of us with good friends and relationships take better care of ourselves. Friends and family encourage us to do so. Having someone to talk things over with, get advice from, yell or scream at, provides an outlet for reducing tension. Perhaps at

no time are friends more helpful than at the crises of life —
birth, death — the comings and goings of people.

You can't wait for a time of crisis, though, to suddenly
look to others for support. So, try this experiment developed
by the "Friends Can Be Good Medicine" project research
team: On a piece of large paper, draw a circle, about the size
of a half-dollar. Put your name on it. Draw smaller circles
around yours. Some quarter-size, some nickels. Fill names in
the various circles as they come to your mind. The names
closest to yours may be the ones that give you the most
support — the ones you are closest to. You may be surprised
with how small — or large — your support group is. These are
key people in your life. Review each name and recall the sorts
of support you have received and given each other. This brief
"charting" of your own support system will help you to
recognize who is important in your life, why, and how you
might strengthen your own "network" of supportive
relationships.

Friends don't come for free, of course. They take time,
effort, being available when you're needed. We all need to
find our own ways to make and keep friends. In one study
reported in *Psychology Today,* researchers found that keeping
confidence, loyalty, warmth and affection, supportiveness,
and fondness were the key ingredients of friendship. What
are the key elements for you? Have you ever considered this?

The facts are clear, according to the California
Department of Mental Health. Friends *can* be good medicine.
The researchers say, "it's time to stop doing business as
usual when it comes to friends. The payoff is not only pleasure
in your relationships but a long-term investment in your
health." Maybe there's more to the saying, "Reach out and
touch someone," than we realize.

Couple's Communication...
You Said What?

Without any doubt, the most frequent reason couples enter relationship counseling is because, "we just don't communicate!"

What once was simple, even enjoyable, now becomes complicated and painful. What was once natural and free, now becomes difficult and awkward.

Let's define the term. *Communication* is the process of exchanging information. That means *everything* you do or say. That also means it is a never-ending process.

Couples who say, "We never communicate anymore" do not really understand what communication is. What they mean is that they don't like the way they relate to each other, or like what they are communicating. Most of their information exchange is probably non-verbal and negative.

If you look at "good" relationships, (no, not Ozzie and Harriet!) you will notice some key ingredients in the way the couple communicates: each is clear about what he or she wants, and is certain the other understands what is being asked. Requests are *explicit*.

You will also notice that positive evaluations of each other are made verbally *or* non-verbally. Negative evaluations, however, are always expressed in words and more specifically as *requests for change*.

Here is an example of a couple that needs to adapt their communication style: She doesn't feel he listens to her when she talks to him, asks him questions or shares her feelings. What does she say? Probably something like, "You never listen to me when I talk to you!" Slam, bam.

His reaction? "You always nag at me!" Slam, bam.

Instead of criticizing or blaming him, she would be better off focussing on what *she* feels. She knows for sure that she "doesn't feel understood." She doesn't know for *certain* that he "never listens" or doesn't understand her.

He needs to take responsibility for his own messages by making "I" statements, and carefully avoid making blaming statements beginning with "you." They are judgemental and simply invite anger.

"I feel nagged!" is quite a different statement than "You always nag at me!"

See the difference? One expresses a concern, feeling or thought you can be sure of — after all, it's your own! The other is demeaning, blaming, and you may very well be making accusations that are incorrect. This leaves the other person feeling unjustly accused and angry.

Avoid the overgeneralizing accusations as well: "You always...," or "You never...." These escalate anger and defensiveness and keep people focused on protecting their positions, instead of concentrating on the real matter.

After spending considerable time with each other, partners get to know each other's buttons, or "hot spots." Some couples find it helps to itemize, or list, the words or phrases that are instant friction between them. Then they arrange a ceremonious "dumping" of these words, and take steps to avoid them. It's unfair fighting if you don't.

"I can't talk about it anymore," is a closed-ended statement that stops communication without dealing with underlying feelings. If you need time-out, ask for it directly — "I'm too angry now, so let's give each other some time to cool off. We can talk more sensibly later."

Effective listening is a fundamental skill many couples need to learn and practice. Facing each other while maintaining eye contact may sound trite, but think about how much eye-contact you and your spouse really have. Are most of your talks done while you are both looking into separate books, a television, or at opposite ends of the room?

Non-verbal reactions — nodding, smiling, frowning — all help communicate that you are listening.

Waiting for the other person to finish speaking before you express your own idea is another sign you are listening. Communicate your specific requests in a timely manner. It may be easier to say, "Last week, I think you made a perfect slob of yourself at the party," but it's a lot more specific — and helpful — to say, "Tonight I would like you to be careful not to spill grape juice on Mary's new white carpeting. I felt embarrassed when you did that."

It's important to offer each other on-going feedback in a constructive way.

While these are a few useful aids in improving communications, by themselves they are at best band-aids for a marriage. Improving the accuracy with which you send and receive messages probably will not in and of itself accomplish all of the changes that you may want in your relationship. It is a necessary step, but not sufficient alone.

I believe in the concept of making the most positive possible interpretation of your spouse's communication. It is too easy to keep the focus on the other's negative messages.

Finally, before you speak, you may want to ask yourself the following questions as guidelines:

- Is what I'm about to say, true?
- Is this a good time to say it?
- Am I being positive and specific?

If the answer is "yes" to these questions, fine. If the answer is "no," why not improve the way you communicate first?

The Healthy Couple

With divorce rates as high as they are today, one begins to wonder whether there really is such a thing as a "healthy couple"!

Nevertheless, research demonstrates that healthy individuals generally tend to gravitate toward other healthy people as partners. These then become "healthy couples," who cope well with what life presents to them.

There are many ways to understand the nature of a healthy couple. The following eight dimensions were delineated by researchers in the late 1970's and early 1980's:

1. What is the couple's "systems orientation" with regard to the external world?

2. What are the "boundaries" between individuals and between generations in a couple and in a family?

3. What kind of "communication" occurs in the couple?

4. What is the distribution of "power" — in other words, who assumes leadership and control in the couple?

5. What is the permissable and expressed "range of emotions"?

6. Are "autonomy and individuality" encouraged or discouraged?

7. Is there a "problem solving and negotiation" approach to handling disagreements and decision making?

8. Does the couple or family have a sense of purpose and meaning in life and a "transcendental value system," or does it feel alienated and adrift in the world?

Regarding a *systems orientation,* couples recognize that they are a unit unto themselves. They each have their own "kettle of fish" and share one between them. They see themselves as definite entities who allow for growth and change between them.

Khalil Gibran, using a marvelous metaphor, described the systems orientation of a couple by noting that a healthy couple is like the strings of a lute. Though they quiver with the same music they are separate and distinct from one another. When they are in harmony as a system they make a beautiful tone. When they are not in harmony as a system, they make an awful sound.

The next characteristic that is described is that of *boundaries*. Here, couples recognize that they are the parents of the children in the family. The children recognize who the adults are. The reverse is also true: when it comes to dealing with their own parents, a healthy couple can let their parents be free to participate in their own activities. Healthy couples are those who have a clear understanding of where they end and other people begin. They are not enmeshed with each other.

Communication in healthy couples is characterized by concordant verbal and nonverbal messages. There are few double messages; desires and expectations are very clearly stated. Their language, when they make requests, is usually in specific, attainable, and measurable statements.

Healthy couples generally have an equalitarian relationship, in terms of *power and control*. Equity and individuality, with little or no coercion or conning are seen in these relationships. There is mutual support.

The healthy couple can express a wide range of *emotions*. Joys and sorrows are discussed, permitted and understood. The individuals can comfort and soothe one another freely. Rather than trying to escape from the problems of living, couples who function optimally confront the difficulties that life presents in a supportive and comforting way.

Love, in a healthy relationship, enhances one's *individuality*, and an ideally functioning couple recognizes that it is this uniqueness and individuality as people which brings them closer together.

Couples who are healthy tend to solve problems through

negotiation, rather than simply compromising or giving in. Compromise always leaves one person feeling like a loser; the ability to negotiate leaves both people feeling that they are winners. Each partner has good verbal skills, as well as the ability to take on issues and to listen in an active way.

A *transcendental value system* is the final variable used to describe healthy couples. There is a clear and shared belief system in couples who are healthy. There is also a deep and abiding sense of meaning and purpose. One finds in these relationships a sense of feeling related to the past and future family history as well as to the world in general.

I offer these concepts in part to measure against your own relationship. At the same time, this may be a way to help you turn major transition events into challenges and to emerge from life's difficulties triumphantly.

Once again, Khalil Gibran: "Healthy couples recognize that they may fill each other's cup, but drink not from one cup."

Love, in a healthy relationship, enhances one's individuality, and an ideally functioning couple recognizes, that it is this uniqueness and individuality as people which brings them closer together.

For My Sister, and Her Husband, On Their Wedding Day

It began with a surprise. But then it always begins with a surprise, doesn't it? It did for me, back in high school, when I turned around to find out who tripped me, and there was the prettiest fifteen-year-old girl I ever saw. Now she's the prettiest thirty-four-year-old I know. And we're still in love.

Love. For you it also started with a surprise. In fact, it was at my surprise birthday party last year that you first met David. There is something unique about meeting at a surprise birthday in a marital therapist's office, of all places. But when it comes to love, it's always unique.

So, your love has grown for each other and everyone around you, family and friends, have survived the past year. In fact, it will be exactly one year. And what a year it's been — watching, sharing, and even encouraging your relationship. What a great relationship you two have. It is really a beautiful thing to see. And in a few days, the important people in your life will help you both celebrate your wedding.

I guess I'm entitled to give you some advice, wisdom and guidance. Not only am I your oldest brother, whom you have honored by asking me to escort you down the aisle, but I'm also a psychologist. And even partly responsible for you and David meeting. Not that you've ever listened to me before, but what can one expect from a baby sister?

But first, the elegant words of Kahlil Gibran, who wrote, in *The Prophet*:

But let there be spaces in your togetherness,
And let the winds of the heavens dance between you.
Love one another, but make not a bond of love.
Let it rather be a moving sea between the shores of
your souls.
Fill each other's cup but drink not from one cup.
Give one another of your bread but eat not from the
same loaf.

Sing and dance together and be joyous, but let each
one of you be alone,
Even as the strings of the lute are alone, though they
quiver with the same music.
Give your hearts, but not into each other's keeping,
For only the hand of Life can contain your hearts.
And stand together, yet not too near together,
For the pillars of the temple stand apart,
And the oak tree and the cypress grow not in each
other's shadow.

Sounds beautiful; so what does it mean? Well, Laurie, I believe it sums up quite well what I've learned from training so many couples whose lives became shattered when "love" faded.

You see, they did not understand that it is the separateness, the uniqueness, the individuality, of each that enriches their union. Genuine love not only admires and respects the separateness of the other, but encourages the other's individuality. Even, at times, at the risk of losing that person.

Some newlyweds so "need" each other that the idea of individual thoughts, tastes, prejudices and desires is terrifying. But inevitably people begin expressing "themselves." Too many get rattled by this, however, believing love must be dying, and believing they made the wrong decision in the first place.

The only foundation upon which you and David can build a mature love is one which allows you both to respect each other's individuality and separateness. It's the only way healthy love, real love, can grow.

Unlike glass, which is rigid, unbending and, therefore, breakable, keep your marriage more like a sheet of cloth. It may get some creases if you're not careful, but it always bends, resiliently bouncing back. It's fragile, and so are relationships.

Assume you each have flaws. And strive to communicate so you can build a lifetime with each other as best friends. But also strive to treat each other as strangers — it keeps the mystery going. And the sex alive.

While sex is a delicate topic, Judaism does have some interesting things to say about it. "To use the conjugal act as a weapon over one's mate, as a means of punishing a mate, or as a means of getting one's way in other matters is a most serious offense in the husband-wife relationship," according to tradition.

David, I also found some other interesting suggestions in our traditional writings. For example, "A man should eat and drink less than his means allow him; should dress according to his means; and should honor — by proper clothing and dwelling place — his wife and children with even more than what he can afford." Further, "A man must love his wife at least as much as himself, but honor her more than himself."

Keep your focus on what's right in your love. It is far too easy to have a counterspy orientation and build a long laundry list of what's wrong. Flaws are less important than your relationship strengths. Everyone argues and has fights. It's worth staying in a relationship despite this sort of stress if you keep a focus on your resources.

Don't try to change each other. It's tough enough to change yourself, let alone someone else. If you want something different from each other, ask clearly for it. There is no shame in direct communication. But be sure you change yourself before you demand that the other change. Act "as if" each of you is committed to the relationship. It's a safer belief, and a more relationship-enhancing one, than the alternative.

It has been said that couples would be wise if they paid for everything in advance in their marriage. If you want something from each other, be certain you are giving it first. "Yesterday is a cancelled check, tomorrow is a promissory note; only today is cash on hand." Keep your perspective on today so you can build for tomorrow. Release what happened yesterday. Don't orient yourself to "emotional bad debts" but to what positive experiences you have today.

You won't have *everything* you want. Bend, yield, compromise and flow. And perhaps more than anything, keep your tremendous sense of humor. You'll need it.

As the song says, "...now you must learn from one another." Congratulations. Mazel Tov. I love you both.

A Funny Thing Happened on the Way to the Bedroom

"Sex without love is an empty experience," claims Diane Keaton in the movie *Annie Hall*. "Yes, but as empty experiences go, it's one of the best," replies Woody Allen.

Sam Levenson recalled a lecture by a sex specialist offering the following advice: Parents should tell their children about sex when they're old enough to understand, and before they're old enough to do what they already did.

Some of you may have had courses in sex education in junior or senior high school. As a parent was quoted as saying, "If the schools teach sex the way they teach everything else, the kids'll lose interest in it."

The statistics on teenage sex, of course, do not support that cynical view. Today, one out of five girls has had sexual intercourse by her first year in high school — almost six times more than in 1948. Each year, a half-million teenage pregnancies end in abortion. Another half-million end in the birth of a baby. Baby to baby — often unwanted.

Levenson again, "The beducation textbooks have turned one of life's prize pleasures into an aptitude test. The failure of either partner in blueprint reading may flunk out a whole marriage." (Wonderful, wasn't he?)

But with all of the emphasis on sex education, with all of the openness on television and radio, with all the liberated couples in their jacuzzis, why all the trouble? The answer of course is very complicated, but I'll keep my comments down-to-earth.

Some couples I see bring to their bedroom a basketful of irrational thoughts about sex. Try these on and see if any feel familiar:

- "Sex is perfect or it's completely dissatisfying." If they don't do it like the couples they see in their rented x-rated movies, something must be terribly wrong. The expectations here are too high. Perfection, whatever that is, keeps too many people feeling they just don't measure up. To avoid the feeling of "complete failure," armed with the knowledge of being unable to be perfect, many simply avoid it altogether. Remember, "If at first you don't succeed — welcome to the club."

- "She *never* wants to; he *always* wants to." Overgeneralizing is also to be avoided. "Never and always" rarely exist (notice I didn't say "never exist"). Keep the focus on when your partner *does* want to. Although it may seem like never or always, recognize how untrue these words usually are. If they are literally true, get some professional help, don't just brood. And if your partner won't go with you, go alone.

• "Anything other than intercourse doesn't count." But who's keeping score? Sex isn't just intercourse. Some of the "sexiest" behaviors have nothing to do with intercourse. What about flirting?

• "It's always the same old thing." So what keeps you from being experimental? One couple I worked with in sexual counseling had an interesting experience. He was afraid to tell her his sexual fantasy and desire, and she was fearful of telling him hers. They were both anxious that the other would disapprove. Guess what? They both wanted to do the same thing; more or less. He on the beach, she in their pool. They learned to be more expressive and communicate more without fear of being criticized for having normal interests. By asking for something specific instead of criticizing what you have, you increase your chances of getting what you want.

Remember, sex is a three letter word — FUN!

Sexual Fantasies

What's normal when it comes to sexual fantasies? That is just what two researchers tried to answer in an article published in the *American Journal of Psychiatry*.

Now, before reading any further, I want you to *honestly* take a look at your own sexual fantasies. What do you mean, you *never* fantasize? Well, for those of you who do or are willing to admit it, how many times per day would you say you think of sex? What is your most commonly occurring fantasy?

Now that you have answered these questions, it's time to read further and see how you compare to the 120 men and women (half of them heterosexual and half of them homosexual) in the research program.

The average number of fantasies per day was about seven or eight, with the range going up to 40 and more. David Barlow, director of the Sexuality Research Program at the State University of New York at Albany, reported that people with sexually-based psychiatric problems, such as rapists and child molesters, have an inordinate number of sexual fantasies each day. Often, it is an obsession for these adults.

Heterosexual men listed these five (in order) as their most common sexual fantasies: a different partner than his wife; forced sexual relations with a woman; watching sexual relations; sex with a man; and group sex.

Heterosexual women ranked these five as their most common fantasies: sex with a man other than their husbands; forced sex with a man; observing sexual activity; romantic sex with an unknown man; and sex with another woman.

Homosexual men listed these five as their most common sexual fantasies: images of the male anatomy; forced sex with a man; sex with a woman; idyllic sex with an unknown man; and group sex.

Finally, homosexual women ranked the following as their most common sexual fantasies, in order: forced sex with another woman; idyllic sex with her established partner; sex with a man; memories of past sexual relations; and sadistic imagery.

Some people in treatment for marital and/or sexual therapy are reluctant to admit having sexual fantasies about someone else while making love to their partners. However, the data and clinical experience suggest such fantasies are quite common and can be useful in understanding something about the nature of the relationship.

If fantasy is used as a way of helping a man or woman become aroused during lovemaking, for example, it can then be a very useful way of increasing intimacy between partners. But if the fantasy is the *only* thing one partner thinks about during lovemaking, it can create distance, not intimacy.

The content can also be quite telling. Does the fantasized person accept you, desire you, admire you, in a way your real partner does not? That may be useful in helping you communicate what you feel is missing in your *real* relationship. Communicate in a positive way, requesting change, not criticizing behavior.

My experience suggests that if you *have* to fantasize about someone else during lovemaking, the real relationship needs help. The key factor is the degree to which you *need* the fantasy to make love.

While most people can admit, if only to themselves, that they have sexual fantasies, rarely are fantasies actually carried out. The compulsive fantasies *necessary* for sexual arousal are generally the ones that are more likely to be acted out. They can also be the most destructive.

Couples who act out fantasies with each other, and with each other's consent, are not necessarily out of the normal range. However, if acting out brings harm, or becomes hurtful against one's wishes, then a problem exists.

Couples in positive relationships can risk revealing something and may grow closer by sharing their fantasies and desires. If you are in doubt about sharing fantasies, use caution. Words, once spoken, can never be taken back. Will your partner be hurt? Can he or she handle your fantasies? Is it important enough to share? These are some of the questions you might ask yourself in deciding if you can grow closer by sharing your most intimate secrets.

Couples in difficulty ought not share sex fantasies unless guided by a trained, skillful marital and/or sex therapist. Communication skills may need to be learned in order to make effective requests for positive change, to avoid arousing defensiveness, and to listen carefully and give helpful feedback.

Many people naively believe something is wrong with them because of their active fantasy life. Some men and women have entered therapy doubting their love for their husband or wife because they have fantasized about sexual relations with someone else while making love to their partner.

When all of the research is complete (and we are far from being there), I suspect the range of normal sexual fantasy life will be even broader than it is today. In the meantime, my aim is to help the guilt-ridden free themselves. Give yourself permission to fantasize — recognizing the difference between thinking something, and doing it. Going to the movies, reading a book, listening to music, watching television — these are healthy outlets for fantasy. And so is daydreaming. Enjoy.

"Was It Good for You?"

Dear Dr. Mantell:
I am 31 years old and have been married four years. For most of my married life I have been having trouble in the most intimate area of my relationship with my husband, namely sex. To be honest about it, much of the time I "fake" my enjoyment. I don't believe my husband can tell, but I believe we have a problem that I am afraid to discuss.

Do you have any suggestions? Also, don't you think that "faking," if I don't mind it, is all right for the sake of keeping the marriage together?

S.R.

The ultimate question which is so often asked between men and women, "Was it good for you?," usually leads to the answer, "Of course!" But for many this may be more a diplomatic and tactful response than a truthful one.

There are times when sexual fakery may seem to be wise in order to protect your partner's feelings, or to help someone save face. The problem in your case appears to be that it has become habitual.

By faking orgasm or sexual enjoyment you are really undermining communication between you and your husband rather than helping it. Once in a while, overstating one's enjoyment may make a partner feel good. When it becomes habitual, it gives a message that says, "What you're doing is fine with me," when in fact it really is not. That will result in him not making any changes, or actually not even being aware of the dissatisfaction you experience.

It's rare to talk about men who fake orgasm, but it can and does occur. More often than not, it involves a man trying to hide his inability to achieve erection by using excuses such as illness or fatigue. Whatever the deception between man and woman, I find the result to be the same: undermining effective communication diminishes your chances to improve your understanding of each other.

Sexual fakery may be only a temporary stop-gap, although in my experience counseling couples, it is usually at the expense of someone's pleasure. Sexual lying is as destructive as any other dishonest communication.

Understanding why you're having the difficulties you are is certainly important. Anorgasmia is correlated with organic causes in less than 5 percent of cases. Primary anorgasmia refers to women who have never had an orgasm, while secondary anorgasmia refers to women who were regularly orgasmic at one time but no longer are. There are women who are situationally anorgasmic in which they have had orgasms on one or more occasions, but only under certain circumstances. Inhibited sexual desire, sexual aversion, or severe, irrational fear of sexual activity may also be present.

While I cannot attempt to offer any individual diagnostic assistance here, it does appear at the very least that communication problems are present. I would strongly recommend considering marital and/or sex therapy. In the meantime, be sure you are looking at sex as an opportunity for intimacy and not as a "job to be done." The communication lines with your partner must be open. There is nothing wrong with telling your partner what you want, in fact it is recommended in sexual therapy.

Among the best advice I've ever heard about sex is not to believe everything you read or hear. Don't compare yourself to what others say sex "should" be like. You must stop pretending that a problem does not exist. Discuss it with your partner in gentle, non-accusatory, non-defensive ways.

If the problem does not go away by opening the lines of communication with your husband, seek professional help. Incidentally, many "sex therapists" have little or no formal training in the area, so select a therapist carefully. Two professional organizations that publish national directories are: The Society For Sex Therapy and Research, Hartford Hospital, Hartford, CT 06115, Telephone (203) 524-2396, and The American Association of Sex Educators, Counselors, and Therapists, 11 Dupont Circle, Washington, D.C. 20036, Telephone (202) 462-1171.

Bedroom Blues – 1.

Doc,
What's wrong with a healthy sexual appetite? My wife thinks I'm oversexed. Let's face it, if she really loved me, she would not be so uptight about sex. If we left it up to her we would only do it once a week. I think she ought to go to a doctor and have herself checked out.

Sound familiar? One of the most common complaints in relationships today, when people are being open and honest, is that one partner wants sex more than the other. When this happens, a number of feelings can result. From disappointment, unhappiness, and frustration, all the way to hurt, anger, and in some cases even marital separation.

Compromise, communication and caring — what I call the "three C's" — usually lead to satisfactory sexual adjustment in relationships. Here, though, I will focus on couples where differences in sexual desire create major forms of marital distress. Most importantly, I hope to offer you some useful ideas on moving towards the "three C's" and eventual marital harmony.

There are a number of well-recognized reasons for a couple to disagree on the amount of sex they want to have. First of all, understand that no one really knows for certain what a "normal amount of sex" is. For some couples, two and three times a day is perfectly reasonable while for other couples once a month or even less may be quite pleasing and fulfilling. Also, let's face it — there are times when a romance is so new and hot that you just can't get enough. As the relationship grows and matures, other things enter into it, which lead to the "honeymoon being over" — and sexual appetites change. This is perfectly normal.

The "averages" that are often reported in great scientific journals (such as *Playboy* and *Reader's Digest*) are just that — averages. What's more, when you read these averages you must take into account the population that is surveyed. Obviously people who read *Playboy* come from a different group than those who read the *Christian Science Monitor*. But the average, generally, for couples in their 30's seems to be somewhere about one to three times per week. How you differ from that does not mean you are under- or over-sexed.

The key is how does your sexual desire differ from your partner's? Perhaps more importantly, how is the difference in desire resolved?

Lack of trust in the other person — and a resulting unwillingness to become vulnerable — is oftentimes a major problem in differences in sexual desire. Negative early sexual experiences are also quite commonly implicated in individuals with problems in sexual desire. In many couple relationships, one partner believes the other has all of the power and control; the only way the powerless partner can gain any control is by deciding when to have intercourse.

Health conditions and medications also affect sexual desire. For example, depression and endocrinological problems are just two such factors that can have negative side affects on your sexual life.

What should you do if you and your partner differ in terms of sexual desire? First, stop blaming the other person. It is important, in fact critical, that blame no longer exists. It is not your partner's "fault" and it is not your "fault." Develop a spirit of cooperation in order to find ways to make your sexual relationship more comfortable and enjoyable.

If you find yourself having a greater sexual appetite than your partner, ask yourself these questions:

• Do I let my partner know that I care for him or her at times other than when I want sex?

• Am I affectionate to my partner in a non-sexual way? Do I give my partner a hug, kiss, and hold his or her hand without expecting to have sex follow?

• Do I share my thoughts and feelings with my partner?

• Do I help my partner feel comfortable and safe with me so that he or she knows that it is O.K. to relax and enjoy things with me?

If you have answered "no" to any of these questions, that should be a guide for you; consider changing the way you are approaching your partner in order to help him or her feel more comfortable being intimate with you.

Sex, quite obviously, is best when you have the time for it. The "quickie" may be fine now and then, but for most people who are excessively tired or rushed, it is quite difficult for sex to be a relaxed and enjoyable experience.

Keep in mind that your sexual relationship is partly an extension of how well you communicate. Try to help your partner communicate to you about what feels good. If you can create a romantic and leisurely atmosphere, and bring some imagination and variety to it, usually sex is experienced as both pleasurable and enjoyable for both partners. If you are the one with higher desire, be sure to focus on your partner's pleasure as well as your own.

You can help your spouse with lower sexual desire by providing an environment that is calm and relaxing; let your partner know that you understand how important it is for your time together to be a haven from the stresses of everyday life.

Bedroom Blues – 2.

Doctor,
He's never satisfied anymore. No matter how many times a week — or even a day — we make love, he always wants more. I mean, what an appetite he has. If we do it twice a day, he wants it three times a day. If we do it three times a day, he wonders why he can't have it four times a day.

Are you the low-sex-drive partner? Well, you have lots of company! Please understand that low sexual desire does not mean necessarily that there is anything "wrong" with you.

Spend some genuine time thinking about how you really feel about sex in general, then more specifically consider your feelings regarding sex with your husband or wife. Is it a neutral experience or do you find it aversive? Are you able to be sexually aroused in general, but when it comes to your partner are simply turned off?

If your lack of desire is related specifically to your husband/wife, then you must give some consideration to how you can improve sex with your spouse. Communication is the key to any good relationship, and sex is much more than simply intercourse and orgasm. Tell your partner what you want, how you would like it, what would make it more relaxing and more enjoyable for you. *Be assertive.* Sex should not become a way to express anger; it is a way to express love.

It may be difficult, but — as in most areas of life — it is far better to focus on what's right with your partner than what's wrong. Has he put on some excess weight? Does she have physical features that you don't like? Work on helping your partner improve those qualities; meanwhile, focus on what is positive. (What you focus on is your choice, not your partner's.)

If your sexual desire in life is *generally* low, consider the following:

- Is your life filled with too much stress?
- Are you willing and able to take time for yourself and look towards your own needs and pleasures?
- Are there things in your life that are making you feel depressed?
- When you do engage in sexual activity, do you enjoy it and wonder why you do not pursue it more often, yet find yourself reluctant to initiate or accept your partner's initiation?
- Did you learn, when you were young, that sex was "wrong," "dirty," or "immoral"?

Compromise, compromise, compromise. When you are the one with the lower sexual desire and you are looking at your partner, it may seem as though he or she wants sex "all the time." Of course, it just *seems* that way from where you sit. So if he wants sex every day while she wants sex every week, a compromise on two or three times per week may be possible. Communication and compromise will go a long way toward improving your sexual relationship. Focus on what *you can do* to make things better, rather than on what *your partner should be doing* — a good thing to keep in mind in any area of marital dissatisfaction.

Finally, if you've tried these suggestions, have communicated openly, have been willing to compromise, but have found that problems caused by the differences in your sexual desire continue, then it may be necessary for you to have professional help. Some couples find that they simply cannot communicate. Other couples find that they simply are too embarrassed or find it too difficult to tell the other person what they want regarding sex. In these cases, marital or relationship counseling will be beneficial — if both partners agree to attend therapy sessions together. Unless *both* of you are willing to change, change is not likely to occur in any meaningful or long-lasting way.

Sexual intimacy, while not the *most* important element of a marriage, is one key to a healthy relationship. It is worth your best efforts to work it out to mutual satisfaction.

Vitamins for a Tired Marriage

Harry and Shirley, who made the air blue with their swearing at each other for almost all of their twenty years of marriage, promised faithfully, in my presence as their marriage therapist, that one would never curse the other again.

"Dr. Mantell, I give you my word of honor, from now on our behavior will be above reproach," vowed Harry as they were leaving my office.

Shirley turned to me. "You really believe what Harry just told you?"

"Certainly. Why not?"

"I'll tell you why, Doctor. I should have so many good years, the number of curses that *momzer* will scream at me before we even get home!"

"Joey, what's the matter you can't bring me a box of candy once in awhile at least?," sniffled the wife. "Before we were married you were always bringing me little presents."

"Sarah, tell me," asked Joey, "does it make sense a man should give worms to a fish after he catches it?"

These two humorous stories capture a great deal of the unhappiness I see among couples today. They promise change but no change comes about. And many couples act as if simply being married will solve all of their problems. That they need to continue to work at it seems a foreign idea to them.

Research has shown that married couples tend to treat each other with much less dignity, tact, kindness and respect than they do total strangers.

Dr. Arnold Lazarus, noted marital therapist and psychology professor at Rutgers University, observes that, "Successful partners aim for conjugal affection rather than romantic excitement, and are sufficiently respectful of one another to realize it takes some effort to keep their mates interested (without succumbing to the notion that this necessarily calls for 'hard work')."

Now understand that one cannot rekindle a dead fire. If the fire is out, *totally out*, you have to build a new fire. When love dies, it remains dead.

If, on the other hand, there is the slightest bit of flame left in the fire, it can be rekindled. If there is some companionship, some conjugal affection, or some sympathetic understanding, it makes sense to try to revive the relationship. But you can only reignite something that has a spark, a glowing ember, left in it.

If your relationship is tired, there are some "vitamins" you can take to perk it up. These "vitamins" are in the form of exercises you and your spouse can do, not an easy pill you can take.

Exercise gives you more energy. So too will these exercises give you marital energy.

First of all, *unity* is an essential ingredient. Unity of goals, togetherness and unity of outlets are all critical. Unless your *attitudes* — at least on crucial aspects of life together — are compatible, a successful relationship cannot be achieved. Learn how to *subordinate some of your individual desires* for the sake of each other. Finally, *common interests* are important for tension reduction.

In his 1985 book, *Marital Myths*, Arnold Lazarus describes a useful exercise he calls the "triple-increase technique." In this procedure, each partner simply makes a list of three positive and specific behaviors that each would like the other to *increase*.

"Don't ignore me over dinner," is negative and vague. "Tell me about your day or ask me about mine, face to face, over dinner," is positive and specific.

Next, check out with each other if the specific and positive items are acceptable to each of you. When you both agree on your lists, then implement them as often as you can.

A cure? No. But a good exercise to get at least six important behaviors written into your new marital script. You need more than one sit-up or one minute of aerobic dance to provide helpful exercise for your heart. Likewise, extensive practice with the triple-increase method can be beneficial for your relationship.

Another useful exercise is one Lazarus calls "prescribed dinners." Set aside one evening a week for the two of you, alone, to go out for dinner. It doesn't have to be a fancy steak house; a sandwich picnic or McDonald's can do just as well. Lavish or budget — it makes no difference.

The point is this is a *regular* commitment you make to each other — alone. Imagine you are dating each other. How do you act? Have you forgotten? Watch other couples, particularly the ones who talk to each other, smile, hold hands, tune out the rest of the world, are playful, attentive, and play footsie under the table. They are dating (or having an affair)!

It is not a place for arguments, quarreling or talking about problems. It is a time for stimulating conversation, encouragement, interest, support and being pleasant with each other.

I've described only a couple of good exercises for revitalizing a marriage that is fatigued. You don't insist that every meal you eat is a gourmet delight, with fine china, crystal, and romantic ambiance. Don't insist that life be a constant four star restaurant. Those of you who demand nothing but a perfect relationship will all too often wind up feeling frustrated and hurt.

You can dream up all sorts of ways of livening up a relationship. You have to begin somewhere, and I believe these exercises are an excellent start for a tired couple. If you find they help, you may wish to get a copy of *Marital Myths*, and read Dr. Lazarus' other ideas about marriage. You may not agree with everything he says, but I assure you it will lead you to examine your own ideas about what a marriage should be.

Good luck!

"Whose Fault Is It, Anyway?"

For some, marriage is the intermission between the wedding and the divorce. For others, it's the way people find out what kind of mates their spouses would have preferred. And for still others, it's the only union which permits a woman to work unlimited overtime without extra pay.

I know that sometimes the romance does go out of a marriage. For some of you, who have been married quite awhile, foreplay is now only a nudge.

One of the saddest sorts of relationships I've witnessed is where each partner believes the other is responsible for the partner's feelings. He blames her for "making" him feel angry. She blames him for "making" her feel upset.

Each points fingers at the other. "You should stop making me feel so unhappy," she says to him. "Me make *you* feel unhappy?" he replies. "You should start making me happy and then I'll stop making you unhappy!"

She responds, "Aha, see, you know you drive me crazy!"

Of course his reply is, "You're already nuts, so I can't drive you that far!"

No, don't get yourself upset. I wasn't tape-recording your argument last night. Or was it the night before?

It's just that this sort of argument is so common, it's easy for some to identify with it rather quickly. Let's analyze one part of it. The part called Blaming.

You see, no one can *make* you feel an emotion. People do things you like, approve of, and agree with. Or they do things, or say things, you do not like, you disapprove of, or don't agree with. *The choice is yours.*

Now, after that, you can *make yourself* feel anger, sadness, joy, sorrow, rage, suicidal or homicidal feelings. These are up to you.

The other person did something, separate from you, of his or her own mind. You can like it or not. It's your choice. And so is the emotion you feel. So you do not have to blame your spouse for "making you feel anger." She only did something. What you feel is *your* responsibility, not hers.

She is late with dinner. "You make me so angry when you do that," he says. But think about it. Did she *make* you angry? No. She was late with dinner. How can that *make* you feel anything except hunger?

He spits in your face. Now while most of us would get angered, he only *made* you wet. Not angry. That feeling, or emotion, you made yourself feel. "You made me angry," makes no sense. "You made me wet," does.

Is this a word game? Not at all. What's the point? Very simply, if you fail to see the difference between, "You *make* me unhappy," and "I don't like that," you will blame your spouse for your unhappiness. You will expect your spouse to fix your feelings. You will expect your spouse to change first so you can then feel happy. You will expect your spouse to have control over your emotions while you throw away your life as a victim. You will also always be angry because ultimately you will resent the "fact" (which *you* created) that your spouse controls you.

Which of course he doesn't. But you have convinced yourself with the nonsensical, irrational lie, "He makes me..."

Of course, being married to someone who blames you, who sees you as responsible for her feelings, is a heavy burden. You walk on eggshells so as "not to upset her," as though you believe the story also, that you *make* her feel an emotion.

Eventually you resent the burden and want to abdicate the responsibility. You act out your resentment in all sorts of childish and devious ways. You don't want the responsibility for your spouse's feelings.

Instead, you want an independent, mature adult to share your life with. After all, isn't that what marriage was supposed to be? Two people, committed to each other, sharing common goals, enhancing each other's growth, sharing intimacies and accepting each other's imperfections. So who said anything about controlling each other?

But that's just what happens when you blame. You give control of your emotions to your spouse, then get yourself angry with him for having it. You upset yourself even more after you've convinced him that he has it!

So stop blaming, and take responsibility. Get yourself angry, wildly upset, joyful, happy, — any feeling you want. But, understand it's your choice and your making. That way your spouse can deal with you by sharing, non-defensively, and help you *get yourself* un-angry and un-upset. The partnership, the teamwork, can work again.

Otherwise, I'm afraid the relationship is destined to become a gruesome twosome — like the couple who had an interesting fight not long ago. She said it was five days since their last argument. He said it was four.

Why Marriages Fail

During the last four months, I learned of three couples I know marrying, and sadly, three couples I know divorcing. What's impressive is how well my experience matches the national statistic. In recent years there have been about one million divorces — and marriages — nationwide each year.

No one argues the fact that relationships are breaking up in alarming numbers. People do argue about why and how marriages fail — especially their own. "He" inevitably enters treatment with a long list of reasons for "his" marriage failing...mostly (if not entirely) having to do with "her" faults. "She," on the other hand, enters treatment with a laundry list of "his" faults.

I've learned that there are as many *individual* reasons for marriages and relationships breaking up as there are couples. But I believe there are four *general* reasons which can be applied to help understand the divorce epidemic:

1. *Background experiences:* Every couple brings to their relationship a set of experiences from their own family relationships. These may often be positive and helpful in learning how to promote a healthy relationship. All too often, though, couples, especially young ones, enter their marriage with either negative or no experience and preparation in the skills required for a positive marriage.

2. *Expectations:* As a marital therapist, I have the privilege of listening to couples' innermost thoughts and

feelings. The expectations and hopes folks have for what love can and should do for them are often surprising. Many relationships that turn sour are comprised of individuals who believe down deep that love should solve all of their problems. They also believe, naively, that love will happen *to* them instead of recognizing that they will have to *work* at it in order to achieve it. The most irrational belief often heard is that, "If I have to work at it, it's not worth having. If I have to ask for it, it's wrong." Nonsense.

3. *Selfishness:* Research reveals that couples tend to treat each other with much less kindness, consideration and tact than they do total strangers. People all too often act in selfish ways towards the people they care most about. Also strikingly noticeable in the failing marriage is that the partners *give* far less than they expect to *receive* from their mates. Think about it for a moment. If the person with whom you're having an affair were to wash your dirty laundry and ruin a prized shirt, you'd probably smile, hug and kiss, say something like, "You're cute and lovable, don't worry about the shirt." *But*, if your spouse of 15 years were to do the same thing, you'd probably explode to the point of having a stroke, blaming, denigrating, screaming and yelling.

4. *Negative focus:* Finally, it seems that people tend to focus on and remember only their problems when things are going poorly, and to forget whatever is positive. Inevitably after the first several sessions of marital therapy, couples still energetically focus on the *one* argument they had in an otherwise excellent, much-improved week. They act as though one negative interaction is more important than several positive ones. They also forget that if they are still together there is usually something good that holds them that way. They fail to see the positive things that occur even in the poorest of marital relationships.

Richard B. Stuart, D.S.W., the noted marital therapist, has developed an approach to marital therapy based on these four issues. Of course, there are no simple solutions for marital dysfunction. Therapy aims to help couples discover, understand, and work on the major contributing factors to their difficulties. It is best done in an atmosphere that is positive and solution-oriented rather than negative and problem-oriented. Specifically, it teaches couples to recognize that by and large their happiness or misery is *their* responsibility. There is *NO* place for blaming when you are trying to mend a broken relationship. Each partner is encouraged to act "as if" the other is committed to relationship enhancement regardless of the actions of the other.

Therapy also teaches that feelings change only *after* behavior does. In other words, *act* in a loving way and loving feelings will more likely develop. Don't wait around for the feelings to be there first if you want to save the relationship.

Finally, focus on improving things in small steps. You can't solve the big problems before you have the ability to resolve little things. Relationships rarely break up over "big" things, but rather over thousands upon thousands of small things, many missed opportunities to express care, and daily small communication problems that grow and multiply.

The Course of Divorce

She's had all she can take. He feels angry, misunderstood and unappreciated. So does she.

And so do their three children.

And their attorneys and marital therapist don't feel much better. Neither do their friends, who have now divided into "his" and "hers," and who are trying to make sense out of what they believe is a senseless situation.

Divorce.

To some, a welcome relief. And to others, as icy-cold as sudden death. But whether divorce has been too long in coming or it is something that comes crashing down on you, it is not an *event*; divorce is a process. Usually long, and usually uncomfortable.

In my work with couples and families going through the emotional strains of this process, I have found that too many do not understand what is happening to them. That lack of knowledge leaves otherwise normal, psychologically healthy people believing that they are going crazy.

"I feel like I'm losing it, Dr. Mantell. We're divorcing but I'm still sexually attracted to him, and yet I hate him," said one woman beginning to face the long process most think ends after the legal documents become "final."

While divorce is not a disease, it follows certain easily identifiable stages, just as a flu might. Knowing what the stages are, and thus knowing what to expect when it is happening to you, may very well make the process easier, more manageable, and leave you feeling more in control.

The first stage is usually *denial*. "It can't be happening to me — it just can't be true!" is the phrase heard most frequently at the beginning.

This turns into *anger* with, "You are an awful _____ for doing this to me!" being the next stage. At times, this can turn into major anger: "You are not only an awful _____ but a horrible monster-abuser-beater-cheat and liar!!"

Depression follows — or may, in some cases, precede — the anger. "I'll never get over this. I'll never get better. I can't do anything to help myself. I'm worthless."

In many couples, actual *mourning* takes place, with the individuals believing that what was sure beats what is. "Of course we weren't happy, but I'm so miserable now, I'd rather go back to the way it was — it sounds crazy, but I miss it."

Accepting the situation allows the individual to move into the final stage, *recovery*. "It's not so bad. I'm surviving even better than I thought I would."

Those are the stages you may very well experience in emotionally separating. Not every couple finds they go through these stages in the same way, at the same time, or in the same order. But to one degree or another, most — if not all — couples describe these feelings as they move from the legal divorce to the final level of divorce, the community divorce.

I'll explain what I mean by "level of divorce." You see, simply having a *legal divorce* in which you no longer have contact with each other is only level number one. This may include serving papers, court appearances, counseling for the children, custody agreements, visitation discussions. But there is a great deal more to the course of divorce.

Next comes the *financial divorce*. The final financial settlement must be reached and executed. If children are involved, as they often are, a plan for their financial future must also be included in that settlement. But that's not all.

The *physical divorce* must be firmly established. Your personal belongings must be in your own dwelling. Your children's needs must also be taken care of in each of your residences. The process continues, though.

Are you *emotionally divorced*? I outlined the stages above (denial, anger, etc.). Have you presented the divorce to your children so they can understand it? Counseling may be very critical in furthering the emotional divorce, especially if children develop problems seeing mother and father, still emotionally attached yet tearing each other down.

Feelings of loss, loneliness, rage, and fear indicate the *psychological divorce* has not fully been finalized. Guilt over "what you've done to the kids," feeling the "single parent blues" are also signs that the psychic divorce is not complete.

Healthy levels of self-esteem — as an individual and as a

parent — indicate the psychic divorce is reaching closure. But the work of divorce is still not complete.

Sexual divorce, which begins so often with continued though less frequent "sex with your ex" and ending with no sexual contact, must also occur.

You must also be *socially* divorced. Your *family* must accept it. You also need to develop a *co-parental relationship* — for the benefit of you *and* your children. Finally, the *community* in which you live must also come to recognize your divorce.

Without feeling comfortable as a divorced person with the family in separate units; without cooperative co-parenting arrangements; and without feeling acceptance of your single-hood within your community of friends, you will not be ready to move on in your life as a committed single or into a new relationship in a genuinely healthy way.

The course of divorce is not an easy one. It can't be rushed, avoided or ignored. It is the prerequisite course that must be passed if you hope to re-establish yourself in a positive, self-assured and confident way.

There is no need to go through it alone. Your friends, family, physicians, clergy and others may be helpful. Professional counseling is often of significant support and should be obtained with no fear of a stigma being attached to it, when it is necessary.

When You Won't Let Go

Nothing lasts forever. Not sorrow. Not joy. Not even life. The good times are fleeting. And so are the bad.

Does that mean the old saying, "Live each day as though it were your last," is a good rule to follow?

Perhaps. But perhaps a better one to consider is, "Treat all the people you meet each day as though it were *their* last."

Nothing lasts forever. Yet so many people hold on to things as though that statement were not true. They especially cling to destructive things. Like anger, hurt and pain.

"But Dr. Mantell, I know you advise me to 'let go' and get on with my life. It sounds good but you just can't understand how badly he hurt me and the children by what he did by walking out on us. I'll *never* let go of my anger towards him."

"Can you believe what she said to me? How do you ever expect me to believe her again? I'll *never* trust her again for as long as I live."

"I'll hate that _____ 'till the day he drops dead. And that can't come soon enough!!"

"She can't stop arguing. Me? I forget it when it's over. She holds onto it forever. I swear she'll die of an ulcer."

These are just a few of the familiar examples that reveal how people allow their energy to be wasted. And how they keep themselves stuck in negativity. And how they throw away precious life time on what was. And how they keep themselves from love.

Were you hurt sometime in the past year and still, to this day, hold the anger? Consider what you are doing to yourself. You see, a person is only destroyed from the inside. But we continue to want to believe *they* are responsible for our misery today — months after the hurt. *They* ruined our world. It is always the other's fault.

How many divorcing couples I have worked with who cling to the ideas of wanting to continue to tear the other down, even months and years after the divorce is final. And how many children still blame parents, even years after a parent's death, for their unhappiness. How much wasted energy, and your precious time, do you continue to invest in hating the teacher who "gave you" the F?

Yet day after day, people hold on. It is as though, if you let go of the hate, anger, hurt or pain, the other person is no longer "wrong." As if you are afraid the other person will be "let off the hook."

The only person "on the hook," though, is you. What do you get out of not releasing your frustration or anger? When an argument is over, it's over. Making someone else's problems yours only makes solving them twice as difficult.

The real shame of not releasing, of not getting yourself unhooked, of not letting go, is that it's a bad investment. You can't change the mistake, the wrongdoings, the hurtful things that were done last week. You can minimize their impact by not clinging to the pain they were meant to create.

Think about people you know who are bitter about things done to them in the past. They are self-defeaters. They are stuck. They appear exhausted, suspicious and retarded in their growth.

Not letting go means a big piece of you is tied up, negatively, in the past. When you try to go on and give of yourself in the present, others around you don't get all of you. Until you let go of old hurts, they linger as new hurts.

The irony, which I see so frequently in divorcing or divorced couples, is that they want the hurtful relationship to be over with on one hand, and yet continue to hold onto it with the other by looking for every opportunity to continue the battle. They just won't let go.

So as you move on with your life, consider letting go. Not only will it be easier for you and those around you, it will be healthier and more hopeful as well.

Part 3.

Your Family

Over a lifetime, our relationships with parents, spouses and children wring us through the entire spectrum of emotions, from love to hate, jealousy to adoration, absolute joy to complete exhaustion, depression and confusion.

How often have we heard the curse of mothers: "I hope you have a child who treats you like you treat me." The amazing thing that I've discovered in my practice over the years is that this curse works!

Often I find adults treat their children as they were treated by their parents without even recognizing it. If people would record themselves talking with their children they might well recognize the same tone, and even the same expressions, their parents used with them. No wonder the relationship between parent and child seems so familiar generation to generation.

Families have a good chance to thrive when parents establish reasonable limits, encourage their children to express feelings, listen to these feelings and, in general, live in an atmosphere of respect.

But that's the real world out your window, and sometimes we need a little help in coping with such things as becoming a parent, dealing with parents as an adult, disciplining children, understanding teenagers, building a good marriage and maintaining a strong nuclear family. It's hard sometimes not to sweat the small stuff.

Twenty years ago, parents contended with long hair; bell-bottom pants; round, wire-rimmed eyeglasses; leather sandals and rock and roll. Today, parents may come face-to-face with a teenager sporting a spiky flat top painted green; shapeless, oversized clothes; rainbow-tinted contact lenses and the incessant shock of heavy metal blaring through the house. Twenty years from now — the imagination boggles at the possibilities.

Through it all, the family remains at the heart of our lives. From the moment of your birth to the last day of your life, many of the most meaningful events in your life, whether joyous or sad, will center around your family.

The following chapters offer a few insights and guidelines to help you understand and handle a variety of family situations and relationships.

Priorities

By the time you learn to make the most out of life, most of it is gone. How sad it is, but I suspect it is all too true for many of you. So the frenetic search for "happiness" begins.

"I've got to find happiness," a husband says to a wife as he leaves. And as the ten-year-old girl asks, "But why do you have to go and move out, Daddy?," he answers, "Because Mommy and I can't be happy with each other anymore, honey. But don't worry. I'll see you soon."

She asks, "When?," to which he says, "Well, I'll see you for two weeks during your mid-winter vacation and you can come visit Daddy for a couple of weeks during the summer."

I don't have to tell you, the chances are she will not see her Daddy again. He will search for happiness. His daughter learned an important lesson. Unfortunately, it is probably a lesson he will deeply regret having taught her.

Sam Levenson asked, "How's the family?" Then he asked, "*Where's* the family?" Then he finally asked, "Where's the *what*?" "Family units are like banks," he wrote. "If you take out more than you put in, they go broke."

I'm afraid the family business is going bankrupt. And all around, people are running every which way, except closer. Meetings, clients, patients, speeches, organizations, classes, charities, luncheons, the theatre, "...planes to catch and bills to pay."

Today's children, and maybe yesterday's, too, are growing up in a fast-paced world. Mom and Pop are out early and home late. That is, if there *is* a Mom and Pop. There are more single parent homes today than at any time in the history of our country. Self-fulfillment? Looking out for number one? The "me" generation? What about the impact on your children?

Like Sam Levenson, who was "not merely family-oriented but family obsessed," I too have come to stand in awe of the power of the family unit. That is clearly *the* central organizer in life. Everything else stands as an imitation. Unfortunately, as the humorist put it, "In current marriages they throw in "till death do us part,' just for laughs."

The ten-year-old girl I described earlier isn't laughing, though. And neither is the little boy who just wants to play catch with his Dad who is too busy. Or the kids in the midst of child custody evaluations all around the country. No, to them it is not a laughing matter. And in the end, it is not a laughing matter to their parents, either.

As I sit day after day counseling families from all walks of life, families who are breaking up, I don't find many who are searching for self-fulfillment, laughing. Many cry. Some pretend to have no feelings at all. Perhaps that is the most tragic.

The seeds planted in childhood sprout in adolescence and mature in adulthood. How many parents come asking how to build a relationship with their eighteen-year-old "stranger," when they never put closeness into the family to begin with? It doesn't happen magically. You have to build a family to have one. And building it means giving up something else. Not personal fulfillment. Not self-development. And not individual happiness. Those that think these are mutually exclusive from family responsibility and joy are sadly mistaken.

Several years ago I was helping a family come to grips with death. An elderly man, in his late seventies, was dying. He was filled with regrets. Most of the regrets were for the times he did *not* spend with family and friends. And his children.

In his half-medicated state in the hospital, he rambled on about trips he imagined taking with his children, things he wished he did with them. Words he wished he said to them. And then he died.

They never went on the trips, they never did the things he hallucinated about, and they never heard the words he uttered. They remembered his professional achievements, dusted off his awards, and argued among themselves as they distributed his money. Sad, but true.

Kahlil Gibran tells us that our children are not *our* children, that they come through us but not from us, and though they are with us, they do not belong to us. He also adds that, "... their souls dwell in the house of tomorrow, which you cannot visit, not even in your dreams."

But we can impact our children, and teach them something about life beyond our achievements, awards and our money. It means changing your life, though, because your values are not taught, they are caught.

You cannot teach or preach values to your children. You can only live them and let your children learn by sharing in them with you.

So, here is a pledge you can make for yourself, your children and your family. It means giving up something you have little of and can't get more of. Time. Give your son or daughter only one hour of your special time per week more than you do now, and watch the return on your investment. Enjoy them, play with them, share with them, talk with them. Only one hour more per week. I can guarantee a healthy growth in your stock.

Cut out a board meeting, another hour at work, a charity meeting. Believe me, when it's all over, the boards, work and charities will go on without you. Your children, though, may not be left with similar feelings. Turn future regrets into present action. If the boards, charities and your banker don't understand your pulling back and investing in your family, ask your children, because they will understand. And if they don't, one more hour won't be enough.

Congratulations, You're Going to Be a Dad!

It used to be that having a baby meant a week or so in the hospital, delivering the child under heavy anesthesia while dad waited — pacing anxiously — in the dingy hospital lounge. Fortunately, it's all different today. Well, *most* of it is different. Expectant fathers still pace anxiously, only now they are often in the delivery room acting as a "coach" — in between their pacing, picture taking, and hand-wringing.

Expectant fathers now also have their own syndrome. It's called "Couvade Syndrome," and morning sickness, weight gain, food cravings, and backaches are all part of the picture. One father-to-be described it to me this way, "When she would eat, I'd eat to keep her company. When she got sick, so would I." His wife said, "I couldn't understand him at all — he was like two different men — one before and one after I gave birth."

Expectant fathers also have a variety of psychological or emotional symptoms, primarily because they are not conditioned for fatherhood. While women have nine months or so to prepare emotionally for motherhood, men are usually expected to adjust practically overnight. The transition from being someone's son to someone's father is a difficult one for many men. There are also not the same bodily changes that women have during pregnancy which make their unique transition real.

Thus it is not unusual for men to feel tense, anxious, depressed, hostile and confused, with ambivalent feelings toward the new baby. Often the couple does not understand these feelings or, worse yet, shares in the denial that they exist. All too often men are given the message, "Just take care of your pregnant wife."

While many expectant fathers channel their normal, healthy feelings into creative and productive outlets like painting, building and other such activities, some fathers-to-be don't handle the pressure or feelings of being neglected as well.

One recent study at Hunter College found that these men instead withdraw into their careers, some become violent toward their wives, and still others turn to alcohol, drugs or other women. Reckless and impulsive behavior is often first seen in men at the time of their wives' first pregnancy.

Expectant fathers may also experience a fear of harming the fetus or their wives. This leads to a decrease in sexual activity which, in turn, makes the wife feel as though her husband finds her less attractive — a feeling she already harbors from the changes in her body.

Pregnancy is usually a time of happiness and joy — as well it should be. Most men with positive self-images and healthy egos survive quite well during the nine months of preparation. For those fathers-in-the-making who don't have a chance to talk about their feelings, it can be an especially frightening and difficult time.

I recommend that couples share their positive and negative feelings. Communication is always a remedy and here it is more important than ever. You see, it may be that he is simply afraid of hurting the mother or fetus. If those sorts of messages are clarified, imagine how much closer you both will feel. If it's difficult for the two of you to share these feelings alone, speak with your obstetrician who may serve as a guide, or refer you to someone else who can.

Psychologist/family therapist Jerrold Lee Shapiro, of the University of Santa Clara, studied over 200 ''pregnant men,'' and wrote about his findings in an article in *Psychology Today*, and a book, *When Men Are Pregnant*. If you wish to pursue this topic further, you'll find both items listed in the References.

The Fifth Commandment

When I was the Chief Psychologist at Children's Hospital, I learned an important lesson from one of the pediatricians on staff. After just being kicked in the leg by a shining example of our nation's future (oy vey!) the child's physician said, "If he kicks you once it's his responsibility. If he kicks you again, it's yours."

Wow, did that make sense. *You teach people just how to treat you.*

Think about what that means. If your husband comes home like a beast and greets you with something less than respect, where did he learn it? O.K., maybe he did learn it from his mother. But how come he believes he can get away with it with *you*?

Because you *taught* him that he could. Of course you didn't stand in front of a classroom and tell him he should mistreat you. No, in fact he probably wouldn't learn it that way at all.

The lesson you taught him was done in a more unconscious, and more effective, way. If you let him do it day after day, and only complain or whine about it, without really doing anything to stop it, then what message have you *really* given him? Namely, that while you will complain he can continue doing it because the "price" is only listening to your complaints.

Perhaps nowhere is the concept of "people will treat you just how you teach them to" more obvious than in parent-child relations. Let's take a look.

In a magnificent book by Miriam Levi (Feldheim Publishers, 1986) entitled *Effective Jewish Parenting*, she discusses the worthiness of honoring and revering one's father and mother — one of the Ten Commandments. Any parent of a basically healthy child knows that youngsters are basically self-centered during their youth. Thus, children generally "lack the gratefulness which would motivate them to honor their parents."

So how do children *learn* to treat their parents with "honor and reverence"? Remember, *people* (including your children) *will treat you just how you teach them to treat you.*

Honor and revere? If the concept is foreign to you, first decide if you want that. If you want it to promote your own personal honor, forget it. If you want your children to fulfill this commandment and its corollaries, emphasize that you want your child to honor and revere "for his or her own benefit."

The time to start is yesterday or today. Not tomorrow. Second, have patience and realistic expectations. Third, you need to have emotional control yourself. Do you model (demonstrate by your own behavior) the behavior you want?

When the youngster misbehaves, as he surely will, your own anger will serve more as an interference than as a help. "The child's behavior is bad for him. Let me see how I can best handle the problem." Sure it is different than the way you normally react ("How dare he speak to *me* that way!"). Expressing hurt or anger, *if* it helps move the child to regret, is useful.

Does your child see you and your spouse treat each other with dignity, kindness, respect and tact? If not, how do you expect your child to react to you differently than the way she sees her father and mother treat each other?

While children have a traditional obligation to treat their parents with honor and reverence, our responsibility as parents is to "create an atmosphere where this behavior comes easily."

If you show your children respect, you are teaching them how they are to treat you. The atmosphere you develop at home is most important. Nothing is a more powerful learning experience than what they see.

Loving concern, sincere respect, patience, moderate demands, following through, beginning at birth, using appropriate punishment — these are all discussed in Levi's book from the perspective of Torah — the Jewish written and oral tradition. I recommend it to any parent who wants to gain some wisdom, learn something about Judaism *and* become a more effective parent.

Natural Consequences

Mother: *"What's the matter, Junior? What are you crying about?"*

Junior: *"Daddy stepped off the ladder and put his foot in a bucket of paint."*

Mother: *"That's funny. You shouldn't cry — you should laugh."*

Junior: *"I did."*

It's very depressing the first time you realize you have a cat that answers to "Kitty," a dog that answers to "Rover," and three kids who answer to nobody.

That's what this article is about. Taking control again. Creating the atmosphere you want with your children using the method of "natural consequences."

I can't promise that if you use "natural consequences" you will be assured of membership into that group of parents with kids who are respectful, studious, intelligent, neat and ambitious. (The group is called the P.L.O. — Parents Lucking Out.)

But if you do use this approach, it will certainly go a long way in promoting self-discipline, emotional maturity and self-esteem while conveying the message of love. It will also help reduce — repeat — *reduce* — strain and stress between you and your children.

Remember first to convey the idea that the reason you bother to correct your children's behavior is because you love them. Tell your children, simply, that you disapprove of their actions, their behavior, but you love them. What they do and what they *are* are kept separate.

In many instances, *conditional love* (not approval or respect) has created more emotional disturbance than any other single life experience in patients I've seen. There is nothing contradictory in criticizing a child's behavior while letting her know how much you love her as a person. Discipline should always be followed by warmth and love.

This approach serves as the basis for the recently-popularized technique called the "one-minute scold." Spend thirty seconds scolding behavior and thirty seconds letting the child know how much you care. It's positive, up-beat and, if used consistently, really works well.

Now to "natural consequences." The room your child lives in is a mess. Do you give the one-minute scold? Do you state a rule that the room be cleaned, and follow through by standing there until it is done?

Natural consequences makes a great deal more sense, and eases the parents' responsibility while not abdicating their role in setting guidelines. Tell the child what you are going to do. Clean your youngster's room one time. Insure the child knows what the standard is by taking pictures of the clean room and posting them so the youngster knows how it is supposed to look. On a regular, daily basis check the room — same time each day. Give fifteen minutes notice before you check it. Whatever items are left out, simply take and lock up for two days, regardless of what the item is, no matter how important it suddenly becomes to your child.

The natural consequences of leaving belongings out in a messy way? Lose them for a couple of days. It is natural, tied to the misbehavior, and teaches self-discipline. *Ignore* the ranting and raving you hear ("But I'll have to go to school with wet hair if you don't give me back my hair-blower!"), and under no circumstances give back the items until the pre-planned time — usually two days.

No need to say, "No television," or "No telephone," or "You have to stay home this weekend," and so on.

The natural consequence breaking a window? Earn money to have it repaired, call the repairman, make arrangements to have it fixed. Does taking the child's bike away have anything to do with the window? What does the child learn?

The natural consequences of temper tantrums? If they are mild ones, ignore them or isolate the child. If they are potentially harmful, restrict the child by holding him or her. Get help if necessary, but don't give in.

The natural consequences of sibling rivalry? They don't stay with each other because they don't know how to be with each other at that time. Separation, cooling off until they can be with each other without fighting, is the natural consequence.

Get the idea? Leaving the bike on the driveway in front of the garage so you can't pull in, is no reason to take away the youngster's T.V. or stereo privileges. Let him move the bike to its proper place, then take the bike itself away, if necessary, for a period of time. That's a natural consequence which makes good sense.

What follows naturally? What is my child learning from this? Am I conveying a message of love in addition to correcting behavior? Am I leaving my child's self-esteem intact?

These are the questions you should ask yourself as you think about your discipline approach. No system is fool-proof. No system *always* works. "Natural consequences" addresses those questions in as positive a way as any discipline approach I've ever worked with. It is designed to build responsibility and control — not simply putting you in control, but building self-control in your children.

Discipline or Punishment

Discipline is not beating up your children, squashing their self-esteem, or coming up with longer and more horrendous forms of punishment. The father who brags that he took his teenage son's driver's license away for three months because the boy's grades fell is teaching very little about improving grades.

And the parents who won't allow their child to watch television for a week because the child used a "dirty word," are probably doing nothing more than creating an opportunity for the child to use a lot more of that language.

I remember hearing a mother of a young child scream at her boy, "Joey, come down from that fence, do you hear? Come down or you'll break your legs. Joey, mommy's telling you NOW! All right, Joey, but when you fall down and break both legs, don't you come running to me!"

Can you imagine what that little guy was thinking? The same parent probably "disciplined" the child for hitting a youngster smaller than him by spanking him while screeching, "This will teach you not to hit someone smaller than you!" Think about that for a moment if you don't understand the point. (And if you still don't understand it, call me and tell my answering service it is an EMERGENCY.)

You see, *discipline* is not the same as *punishment*. Discipline teaches self-control and builds conscience. Punishment teaches that you are bigger and stronger.

Discipline builds a collaborative atmosphere. Punishment builds a tense authoritarian atmosphere. There is certainly nothing wrong with authority. Kids need it. So do adults. But punishment too often leaves children feeling as if *they* have been rejected, whereas discipline conveys the essential message of dissatisfaction with the *act* which was committed.

Research over the years has shown that punishment may stop unwanted behavior for the moment, but all too often it only teaches not to do the behavior when the punisher is around. It pushes the behavior underground. It usually does not stop it.

Now, if you are the kind of parent who needs to bully, then your children or spouse are probably easy targets. The more you punish — instead of discipline — the more you will need to do it. Since punishment creates more need for you to punish — as it does not really stop the behavior — you insure a great system for yourself. Little punishments won't work, so your child will again misbehave. You catch them in the act, punish again and so on till adolescence — when you throw your hands up altogether.

This negative cycle is as troublesome as the complete opposite — parents who are so insecure that they can't bear the idea that their children won't approve of them, so there is no discipline at all. The absence of discipline equals the absence of guidance.

Whereas secure, loving parents are not overly upset at the inevitable, ''I hate you Mommy and Daddy,'' insecure parents have a different reaction. Either they submit to the child's extortion-like threats and make nice to the true ''leader'' of the family, or they become so enraged that they have to beat that feeling out of the child, ''This will teach you to not hate your Mom or Dad.'' Oh really? Guess again.

The concept of ''modeling'' has to enter here. It reminds me of little Billy's grandfather who was something of a philosopher and never missed an opportunity to give out bits of sage advice to his grandson.

"Yessirree, Billy," he said one day, "remember fools are certain, but wise men hesitate."

"Are you sure, Grandpa?," the boy asked.

"Yes, my boy," said the old man, laying his gnarled hand on the child's head, "I'm absolutely certain."

The absence of limits, firmness, or guidance, and the unwillingness to discipline are as responsible for rebellion against parents as overly punitive reactions. Parents are often shocked to hear in my office, from their children who are brought to me for misbehavior, that the children feel mom and dad are too lenient.

Children know when parents are afraid to discipline. Of course they won't tell you that unless an atmosphere of listening is created.

Stick with firm, consistent, loving discipline; you won't need to punish.

Thumbsucking

Dear Dr. Mantell:
My child is nine years old and continues with a habit I believe
she inherited from me — thumbsucking. I was an active
thumbsucker until I was a teenager and finally grew out of it.
But it was so embarrassing. I absolutely do not want my son to
have to go through it. We've tried it all, from obnoxious
dental appliances to Tabasco on his finger. Nothing's helped.
Any suggestion would be sincerely appreciated.

Mrs. L.E.

Dear Mrs. E.:
Thanks for your letter. Thumbsucking is a common habit;
even Linus sucks his thumb in the "Peanuts" cartoon strip.

Actually, the statistics are quite interesting. About 40
percent of one year olds, 20 percent of five year olds, and five
percent of ten year olds continue to suck their thumbs. Of
those who are chronic thumb-suckers, about half stop by the
age of eight, and all but ten percent stop by the age of ten.
And the research tends to find more female thumb-suckers
than male. No *one* cause has been established.

Research *in utero* shows that some infants suck their
thumbs prior to birth. There is *no* data to suggest that
thumbsuckers are more emotionally disturbed than
non-thumbsuckers. It's pleasant, relaxing, restful, and
reduces anxiety.

When the child finds other ways of gaining security or
pleasure, it's quite likely the habit will stop. Until then, as a
parent there are a number of things you can do to encourage
this gradual process.

Understand that if you simply sit back and let it continue,
especially in your nine-year-old child, the continued risk of
dental and oral malformation is quite significant. If the
thumbsucking stops before the child's permanent teeth have

erupted, that is before age five or six, any malocclusion will tend to correct itself. But if thumbsucking continues after the permanent teeth erupt, the jaw muscles and bones can be seriously affected.

Dental malformation aside, the thumbsucker tends to daydream frequently, withdraws from the world, may have special problems develop, and may very well face social trauma.

So, you've tried the pacifier (in a child three or younger, especially the new shaped model which conforms to the shape of the mouth); you've been tolerant; you've provided all the security in the world; you've allowed increased nutritional sucking time for your infant or toddler — and your child *still* sucks her thumb. Here's what to do:

• Try ignoring it. Remember the statistics — most children give it up by age five or six. Ignoring it can help keep it in a proper perspective and not make it a big issue, thereby creating a power struggle. In addition, if the thumbsucking is a symptom of an underlying emotional issue, ridding your child of the ''smoke'' won't stop the ''fire.''

• ''Ignore'' doesn't mean ''do nothing.'' Insure your child's sense of well-being, reduce stress in the family, avoid unnecessary criticism and open the lines of communication. Offer alternate activities to occupy the child.

• Hands-on activities such as play-dough, clay, and other art materials can prove useful.

• Avoid shaming or yelling or threatening. I *strongly* suggest that you avoid the use of mechanical restraining devices, though they are almost 100 percent effective. Short-lived side effects such as speech difficulties, increased mood disturbances, sleep and eating problems are common.

• Offer some education to the older child who continues to suck away while in kindergarten, first grade or even beyond. Let him know how it can affect the mouth. Let him know you are unhappy about the habit and offer several suggestions to help the child break the habit.

- Avoid shaming or force — you may be paying far too expensive a price to stop a habit. By being harsh, forceful or overly shaming, you will create a much larger problem than a habit that needs retraining. You may well be adding to a growing sense that your child feels misunderstood, ridiculed, and perhaps even unloved.

- If the child is observed thumbsucking, gently but certainly take the thumb out of the child's mouth or distract the child.

- Try a system of rewards or mild penalties. Restrict sucking to a certain place and time. Bed-time or nap-time is most common. Check on the child at other times and use a star or point system for rewards with prizes easily and quickly attainable. Catch the child not thumbsucking, and reward. Make a game out of it and have fun. Penalties may include turning off the TV for a specified period of time, stopping the reading of a book for a five or ten minute period, or other withdrawal of pleasurable activities in which the child is engaged at the time. So if you're reading to your child (remember that? Parents need to read more to their children!) and he's sucking away, put the book down for awhile, then come back to it.

- Chewing gum, sugar-free of course, lolly-pops, or other socially-accepted sucking substitutes are often helpful. Restricting the child's favorite thumbsucking blanket or toy to a specified room may serve as an excellent distractor and help limit the sucking to one place.

- Social pressure can be an excellent way to curtail the habit, especially if it is positive. That is, upbeat, positive comments from family and friends when the child is *not* sucking can be most beneficial. Don't make a public "spectacle" of the child, however. Embarrassment may be counterproductive.

- I have found bed-time "suggestion" in the form of mild hypnotic-like messages especially helpful. Telling the child over and over again in a story or song that he will "grow bigger and eventually stop sucking his thumb soon'' can be surprisingly effective when done at a restful, quiet time as sleep settles in. A sing-song, monotonic voice is helpful, but avoid a stereotypic hypnotist's manner. It is subliminal, not explicit. By telling stories about other children, or yourself, who have stopped, you are offering positive hope.

• Some books on the market are also helpful and can serve as good role models:

Ernst, K. *Danny and His Thumb* for ages three to seven.
Fassler, J. *Don't Worry Bear* for ages three to six.

• Finally, if you've tried it all, contact your pediatrician, dentist, or a mental health professional who specializes in working with children and their unique habits.

"Mommy . . . Look What I Made!"

Dear Dr. Mantell:
I recently attended a lecture you gave on parent-child relationships and was too embarrassed to ask you this question in public. My pre-school child is forever bringing pictures, projects and other arts and crafts things home from school. He has come to see the refrigerator as a big picture frame where he can proudly display his creations. The problem is my husband — or rather his reaction to my son's productions. I just can't get him to pay attention to our little boy's efforts. Any recommendations?

Mrs. C.K.

What parent hasn't seen a child gleam and beam with pride saying, "Mommy, Daddy, look what I made," or "look how well I can read (write, ride my two-wheeler, etc.)" It sometimes seems that child's play is solely designed to enhance their self-esteem. Guess what? Much of it is. If you observed the number of times a day your son or daughter engaged in play that's at least in part self-enhancing, you'd be surprised.

Your husband may unknowingly be depriving your son of opportunities for developing a sense of mastery and good feelings about himself. At the very least, encouragement and reinforcement — necessary for *all* children — are missing.

To master the environment, and to gain positive self-esteem and a sense of competence are crucial needs of the developing child. I believe them to be among the most important issues — perhaps the most important — a youngster can take out of pre-school into public school.

It begins early in life. Think about your infant who would rather feed himself than have you feed him. The two- or three-year- old who "practices" separating from you to assure himself he can — and that you'll still be there. The pre-schooler who wants to dress herself. These are all examples of striving for self-esteem.

And what do many folks do in response? It's quicker, less messy, and easier to do it yourself — so you do. But at what price? None, if it's not a chronic occurrence. But if you *always* want to avoid the mess or a few moments of waiting, and never let your child take the risk, the price is quite expensive: your youngster's self-esteem.

So what do you do when you hear, "Daddy, look at what I drew?" React positively. Sure it may be a pain in the neck. Raising healthy children isn't always a slice of heaven. Nor *should* it be. It might be nice if we could just conceive them and never have to change a dirty diaper. But a loving relationship requires sharing tough times as well as fun times.

Compliment the picture, writing effort, skill and product. "What a great alphabet!" is effective. "You're a great kid for what you did!" is *not*. It's not reasonable to rate a whole complicated *person* based on one production. It *is* very appropriate to rate their traits, performances, skills and abilities. What one *does* never, ever enhances or detracts from one's basic value as a human being. Unfortunately we tend to believe irrationally "I *am* better if I perform better, and I *am* a worm if I act wormily." It's one heck of a message to give to your child. Avoid it.

If you do not, perfectionism may soon develop — with a host of other symptoms following along. Keep in mind that compensating for feelings of inadequacy is one of the key reasons children (and adults) develop psychological difficulties. Certainly, it's not the *only* one, but it is often a culprit. Children who lie and exaggerate are often youngsters who basically don't feel good about themselves. They think they have little to offer that's worthwhile, and irrationally believe if someone outside approves of *them* they actually *are* better.

There's a difference between extrinsic and intrinsic worth, however. All of the compliments in the world to a young child who doesn't believe she's attractive, will not make *her* feel she is. Children do well to learn they are worthy of your praise to a specific act. By keeping the praise focused on their performance, skill or production, you will go a long way in enhancing self-esteem. But keep their performances (extrinsic worth) separate from their value as persons (intrinsic worth).

Let's assume you have just lost your job. *Anxiety* about it stems from believing in perfectionism, that you *must* live up to others' standards, that it's awful if you don't, and that your self-worth is now decreased. Ask yourself, would you actually become worthless as a human if you *did* lose your job? Of course, you wouldn't. At worst, you'd be someone who didn't do well on that job — but worthless? Hardly! Rate your traits, performances and abilities if you must, but leave your *self* out of it.

Deal with your children in the same way. There's a great deal to using your refrigerator as a frame for a child's drawings. Praise for a child's small achievements can be a valuable self-esteem builder. It means a great deal more to your child than perhaps your husband realized. It's *never* too late to change — especially for your child.

Mental Health in Children

The little Swiss village, high in the Alps, was having its troubles. Novices were invading the most difficult slope and the results were catastrophic. Injuries and even fatalities were mounting. The townspeople met together to decide what to do. As the story goes, the men and women of the village decided to invest in an ambulance to station at the base of the slope to pick up those unfortunate skiers who did not make it.

While an ambulance may be helpful, fencing off one dangerous slope to prevent access might well have been a more sound investment. This article has as its focus, fences and not ambulances — that is, ways of promoting mental health in children.

Mental health professionals have traditionally considered healthy human functioning as the absence of psychological or psychiatric disturbance. In other words, health was the lack of disease.

More recently, humanistically oriented theorists have begun to redefine mental health in terms of the presence of social and personal competence. In fact, one of *the best predictors of absence of adult mental illness and maladjustment is the presence of various forms of competence and ego maturity (in childhood) rather than the absence of problems and symptoms.*

There are as many definitions of mental health as there are professionals writing about it, of course. Yet another view of healthy human functioning is the freedom to make choices without being burdened by irrational thoughts, fears and fantasies, or constrained by outside stresses.

A useful story often told by family therapist Salvadore Minuchin deals with the travels of a North Pole adventurer. It seems that on one of the coldest days of the year, with snow, sleet and ice abounding, the traveler began a 20-mile journey northward. After an extremely trying, strenuous and physically exhausting trek in the worst of foul weather, the traveler at the end of his journey checked his compass. He was astonished. The compass indicated that he had *not* traveled 20 miles north but actually was 10 miles south of where he began! He woefully reasoned that while he did in fact travel the distance of 20 miles that same day, he was doing it on an iceberg which was traveling south faster than he was traveling north!

As Minuchin's story illustrates, an individual therapeutic intervention in one direction, while the "family iceberg" moves in the opposite direction, can leave an individual in a similar situation to our North Pole traveler — having put in a lot of effort with little progress. The point is that *the family is the central agent for promoting individual mental health in children.*

What characteristics does the healthy family give to its members? Here are some of the positive emotional factors families can develop: self-worth, uniqueness, responsible and direct communication patterns, cognitive and emotional competence, capacity for positive growth and change, and a solid foundation for moving outward into society as a productive participant.

There are a number of valuable ways of observing family functioning. One system suggests the following framework for thinking about family tasks which serve to promote mental health and competence:

An initial task of the family is that of promoting *identity formation*. Every individual has a need for both a sense of belonging and a sense of individuality. Families which promote the mutuality of being a part of a group with shared heritage and experiences are taking important steps towards facilitating mental health, as long as they also encourage independent self-expression. At the same time, there are those families in which members are isolated, with no sense of emotional bonding. And there are some which are enmeshed: so close that they prevent individual expression and do not allow for privacy.

Coping with change is another crucial task in the life of a family system. The healthy unit is flexible in its problem solving methods, adapting to day to day strains in ways which are highly effective. The life of a family is filled with stresses, of birth, death, a youngster going off to school or college, moving, a new job, unemployment, and more. Children become secure when some degree of predictability is afforded them by parents who meet life's problems with flexibility and stability. On the other end of the continuum are families who, for a variety of reasons, use the same problem solving methods for all stressful situations. There is little in the way of flexibility and thus very likely poor problem solving. In addition, there are those families who lack any source of stability, and instead function in a haphazard, disorganized manner, resulting in chaos and confusion during times of stressful change.

Information processing, or communication skills, is another critical task in the life of a family. It is impossible not to communicate something in a family group. On the positive side are those families which foster an atmosphere in which people are encouraged to express their thoughts and feelings

— "good or bad" — and to be heard. Messages are given and received in clear, uncluttered and specific terms. Family members not only listen, but hear and acknowledge. The age-old "telephone game" where one person communicates a message to a second who passes it along to a third, etc., etc., serves as a useful model for what can happen with unclear information processing.

Each family, knowingly or unknowingly, maintains a system in which members fulfill certain *roles* or functions. Family members are most comfortable where these roles are spelled out carefully, parents are clearly in charge, and children live with consistent and clear expectations in their daily lives. In these homes, generational lines are well established and the parents' role as parenting agents is firmly grounded. On the other hand are those families in which "you can't tell the player without a scorecard" — children are parents, parents are children, and no one seems to know who is supposed to do what.

The point of this brief article has been to highlight one way of thinking about psychological health in children, in which the absence of symptoms is less important than the fostering of positive ego strength and competencies. I firmly believe that the family is the single most important institution in fostering positive mental health. There are a number of critical tasks for the family; I've outlined a few here, including the importance of *identity formation, coping with change, information processing,* and *role structuring*.

There are a number of agencies that specialize in treating families, including Family Service agencies in most communities. Your pediatrician or family practitioner can refer you to a therapist in private practice as well.

Improving Your Child's Self-Esteem

Have you ever wondered to yourself, "I wish I could get my child to feel better about himself"? So, as a kind, warm, loving parent you invent all sorts of ways to boost your youngster's self-esteem.

That may include making sure he has the "best" clothing, the most expensive sports equipment, telling him he "is the best," and giving him smiley stickers and other rewards every time you possibly can. Emotional uppers.

All very nice except that, unfortunately, the message you give your child may very likely backfire on you. Oh, the short-range goals will certainly be accomplished. But as soon as your child meets up with someone who doesn't happen to think of him as "Moses reincarnated," what skills can your child bring to bear on the situation?

Here is a true story to illustrate what I mean. Several years ago I was treating an attorney for severe depression. So severe that this "successful" lawyer had attempted suicide and was racked by anxiety.

He would say things to me like, "I can't do anything right," "Nobody I know really likes me," "My partner makes me so mad — he just ruins my whole day," and "I'm no good — I haven't won a case in the last six months."

Because he believed he was not a good lawyer, he believed he was not a good person. For him, being a good lawyer meant being a good person.

Well, several months into the therapy he came in and said, "Dr. Mantell, I believe I understand it now. Today I kept telling myself I am the best lawyer in town and, I gotta tell you, I just felt great about myself."

Like a splash of icy water, I told my dear depressed patient that he did not *quite* have it.

You see, self-esteem doesn't come from believing you *are* the best or from believing you *have* the best. That is much too fleeting. Our lawyer, by his logic, would fall into the pits if he lost his next case. Self-esteem comes from within, not from without.

In order to genuinely improve your children's self-esteem, you must teach them skills, knowledge, and a process for controlling beliefs regardless of what goes on outside. There just are not enough smiley stickers, and as many sadly find out, there never will be.

"I can't do it," "It's too hard," "I never do anything right," and "I'm no good." Do these sound familiar? Real-life phrases uttered by real-life children. Maybe your children.

But these negative self-statements, "junk thoughts," are not the phrases of malignantly depressed children. They can be heard, if you listen carefully enough, by many youngsters with less than favorable self-esteem.

In improving your children's self-esteem you have to teach them the difference between physical pain and emotional pain. With physical pain, the source is always clear. A brick falls on your foot and it causes the feeling — pain. But when your youngster experiences emotional pain, you have to teach him the idea that what happens (for example, being called "Shorty") does not *cause* feeling angry. Rather, your child must learn that in experiencing feelings and emotions he has a choice: not everyone feels the same way when he is called "Shorty." Different people may have different feelings.

Teach your youngsters that when it comes to emotional pain, what happens does not cause the feeling. Something else causes emotional pain. They must learn that *thoughts and beliefs about what happens cause feelings*.

I have led small groups for youngsters to help them raise their self-esteem. These groups of six to eight children focus on teaching children how to get rid of their "junk thoughts" and to replace them with more appropriate thinking about the outside world. Working with these children I find four kinds of major thinking distortions which underlie much of their unhappiness and self-esteem problems.

• The first is *"should" thinking*. This belief, that people, or ourselves, or the world should be a certain way or should be different than it is, is a major culprit. The child comes out with the following kinds of phrases. "People have to be *nice* to me!" "That's not *fair!*" "I just *have to* win the race!" "You *should* not do that to me."

• A second sort of irrational thinking that children with poor self-esteem have is *blaming*. Whenever your child refuses to take responsibility for herself, it comes out in the form of, "It's not my fault!" "He made me do it." "You make me so angry!" "If it weren't for my teacher, I would get better grades." If these children continue to wait for everyone else in the world to help improve their lives, they may be waiting a very long time. Further, they will always attempt to change everyone else in the world, which of course they cannot do, thus leaving them feeling miserable and unhappy.

• The next sort of thinking distortion is called, *over-generalization*. "Everything bad always happens to me." "Nobody likes me." "I'm the only one who doesn't have a brand new bicycle." "I always get in trouble." Words such as *always, never, all, none, nobody*, or *only* pop up in this category. Also in this category comes labeling. Labeling an entire person because of only one thing that they do or say is just as much an overgeneralization as is taking a little bit of information and making a big deal out of it. So, for example, when you insist that your child do his homework, he labels you as "mean."

• The fourth sort of erroneous thinking style is *catastrophizing*. "Not getting the birthday present I want is *horrible!*" "I just *can't stand* the thought of not going out on Saturday night!" Words such as *awful, horrible, terrible*, and *catastrophic* fall into this category.

What you must teach your child, and what we do teach youngsters in our group counseling program, is that demands, cop-outs, overgeneralizations, and catastrophizing are just beliefs, not facts. A fact is that it is raining outside. That is what is happening. The child's feeling about the rainy day may be happiness or sadness. The feeling doesn't come from the fact that it is raining. Instead, your youngster must learn to understand that he or she has beliefs about what is happening. One youngster may say, for example, "Wow! It's raining here. That means it must be snowing in the mountains. That's great — I can go skiing, and I don't have to do the yard work I promised my parents I would do." Another child may say, "How awful, horrible and terrible. Whenever I want to do something, it always rains. I'll never be able to ride my bike because it will always rain."

Your youngsters must learn to understand what their thoughts are, and understand them as beliefs about actions.

Improving self-esteem is a lifelong task. Children must learn that outside events do not disturb them as much as their own beliefs about those outside events do. Some public schools are beginning to provide small group counseling for children to learn this sort of emotional curriculum.

If you have further questions about self-esteem building, check the references for this section, or contact your child's school guidance counselor or another mental health professional.

Working Parents

It seems that parental concerns are seasonal. In the summer, moms and dads worry about how best to fill their little one's time. Is he or she ready to go off to camp? Should he have extra academic tutoring to give him a head start in school next year? What if she wants to spend all of her time at the beach?

Once school begins, a prominent concern I have come across is the dilemma of the "working mother." No doubt many of you who work out of the home with school-aged children will be called on to become involved with PTA, be a class mother, serve as Girl Scout troop leader, coach a team. If work keeps you from being as involved as you'd like, it probably generates some degree of guilt or anger when your child says, "But mom, all the *other* moms are doing something!"

Is it really necessary for your child's well-being to get involved in these school activities?

While I don't think it is *absolutely* necessary to involve yourself in these kinds of activities, trouble *can* begin if your child comes to feel that your work is more important than he or she is.

Historically, Mom was at home. For better or for worse, she was always within earshot of her youngsters. And she was tuned in. With sixty-five kids playing in the street, if one yelled, "Hey, Ma!" only one "Ma" — *that* kid's mother — would stick her head out and answer, "What now?"

Things are not so easy these days, of course. Attitudes about women working have changed. *Most* young mothers work outside the home, many in highly specialized jobs. Ma may commute a considerable distance in order to work in her chosen field. It's tough to hear your child's "Hey, Ma!" from East Suburbia when you're in an office building in Center City! What's more, she may participate in community activities, attend an exercise class, or have shopping to take care of *after* work.

While it may not be quite like that, if your child feels you are too busy to offer positive attention, he may learn all too fast that by doing poorly — either at home or in school — he certainly can get your attention. Your youngster may then be unconsciously testing you to see the degree to which you are genuinely concerned about his life in and out of school.

So what do you do? First be sure to reassure your youngster that your decision to go to work (and it *is* always a choice) is *not* a rejection of her. Provide your child with the assurance that if she is ever ill, you or someone else will definitely be there to care for her. Be sure she knows how to reach you if she ever needs you right away — and test it out with her so she knows she can in fact get to you. If you can't arrange your hours to be home when your child returns from school, try to arrange some sort of after-school activities for her. If that's not possible, a phone call from work may be all that's necessary to let her know you care and are interested in her day.

While most children adjust well to working moms, if you read your child's behavior carefully, you'll know if more of your involvement is needed.

When Your Child Starts School

Each fall, tens of thousands of young children throughout the country face a milestone in their lives: the first day of school. As parents, many of us wonder where the last four to five years have gone. After all, wasn't it yesterday that the little genius took her first step, uttered his first word, finally got toilet training down pat?

As Tevye sighed in *Fiddler on the Roof*, "...seedlings do turn over night to sunflowers, blossoming even as we gaze." But is your child ready for school, and what can you do as a parent to help ease the way? Your understanding at this very important turning point in your youngster's life is critical to his future attitude toward school, learning, and to his psychological growth and development. In my experience, teaching children to read early, giving them a home computer at four years of age, or other such riches are not the things that get a child ready for school; it's the cutting of the cord from the parent that does it most effectively. The cord needs to be snipped away, a strand at a time, but not before the youngster is ready. Next to holding a child back, nothing hurts a youngster more than to hurry her up.

One educator put it this way, "A parent's job is to teach the child how to cope with his life. At home he learns the 'life skills' that transfer to the classroom; to cook, to clean up after himself, to be punctual, to behave with company. He learns to say what he means, to be direct when feelings should be spoken."

Unfortunately, as Marie Winn pointed out in her book, *Children Without Childhood*, many middle-class youngsters in this country have been robbed of their most precious birthright — childhood itself. They've been pushed to grow up quickly — often too quickly — as a result of such social factors as the sexual revolution of the 1960's, spiraling American divorce rates, and sweeping changes in the economic and social status of women. Attitudes about children have changed as well, and many adults feel that it is unfair to demand that children be in submissive or deferent roles. Others, however, believe that "new-era child-rearing" — in which the youngster is seen as an equal partner in his or her own upbringing — has turned out to be rather disastrous. We know that youngsters do not do well when they are treated as adults. Children require the security which is a part of being dependent and unequal.

So what is the adult's responsibility in preparing children for the beginning of school? Here are some things for you to keep in mind:

• Recognize that the first day of school for your youngster is a very important event. For many children it's the beginning of a new universe of friends, learning and adventure. The greatest gift you can give to your child is your loving support and understanding. Make the first day of school an event to be celebrated, even if the child attended pre-school.

• Remember that learning to like school and liking to learn are closely related. The more positive the information your child has about school, the more the child will want to participate in school. If her big brother or sister says that school is fun, that will help. If mother and especially father emphasize the usefulness and importance of education, that will also be of use. If the beginning of school is not celebrated or is seen as unimportant and trivial, the youngster will surely pick up on that.

• Prepare your youngster for the new school experience by explaining what to expect and answering all of his questions honestly. A visit to the school and perhaps even meeting the new teacher in advance can often be helpful.

• Convey a positive attitude about school.

• Make transportation plans very clear to your child. Create a normal, routine atmosphere at home the first few days of school. It's best not to deny or avoid the uniqueness of the situation, but take and active interest in what your youngster is telling you about school when she comes home. Allow time to talk about school and the child's new friends there.

• Give your child free play time at home — it will be needed now that his school day is going to be so structured.

• Be sure you get to know your youngster's teacher. If the school has a Parent-Teacher Organization, volunteer your services and become involved. It shows your youngster that you care enough about what goes on in her world to take time from yours.

• If at all possible, plan your day so that you can spend some time with your youngster at the end of each school day. This is not always possible, but it certainly can be made up with a phone call, a note that you leave for the child to find when he comes home, or some other way to let the youngster know that you are thinking of him.

• It's often best to let your child settle the quarrels or difficulties that may arise with school friends. Usually, unless the children are harming each other physically, it's wise not to rush to the rescue.

• Avoid comparing this child's school experiences with how brothers and sisters or neighbors did when they began school. Comparisons such as this can be potentially harmful to your child's self-image. Everyone is different and everyone meets life's turning points and experiences in her own way.

• Your job is to support and help your children's development — not to protect them from a world about which they must learn.

• Finally, recognize that if problems are apparent, it's not necessarily because of parenting skills. Some children may simply be difficult youngsters. Some kids are fortunate enough to have regular habits, enjoy new experiences, be adaptable and positively-oriented. But if youngsters are slow to warm up, or ''mixed'' in their temperament, adjusting to school may take weeks or even months. Youngsters must be accepted for themselves; after all, they are expected to live out their own lives, not necessarily their parents' dreams.

Your youngster will never have a first day of school again. If you look back over the last four or five years of your youngster's life with regrets for not having spent time, for doing too much or doing too little, rewrite the memories you will have in the future by changing your approach today.

Bad Grades, Good Children

Dear Dr. Mantell:
Our two children are 10 and 14 years old. The younger one
always does well in school, while the 14 year old has had a
history of learning disabilities, and with the problems, he gets
more than his share of poor grades. My husband and I do not
agree on the best way to react to the 14 year old's bad report
card. Any thoughts?

You remind me of the father I recently spoke with after
one of my lectures. He told me he was suffering from a
low-grade infection. "Every time I see my son's report card,"
he said, "I get sick!" I can certainly understand how he feels.

When I was a kid we used to write the answers to
questions on our fingernails. One time I got so nervous, I
chewed up two years of intermediate algebra!

The report card arrives, and you take a look and feel as if
you're going to explode. What do you do?

Well, if you want to help *insure* poor grades in the future,
simply get visibly upset, upsetting your youngster. Or punish
your child, or promise rewards for getting good grades, or just
seethe.

If you want to *help* your youngster achieve better grades,
try a low-key approach, praising what your child did that was
positive, encourage her to do better in those areas she needs
to improve in, and offer some help (perhaps a tutor).

This advice carries from a recent research project
involving almost 8000 students in six San Francisco Bay area
high schools. The project was headed by Dr. Sanford M.
Dornbush of Stanford University. The research involved 3500
parents and 500 teachers.

Low-key encouragement will not be sufficient to combat a *totally* poor report card, according to Dr. Dornbush. These children need professional help. The school professional (guidance counselor) is the place to begin, then go on to educational or clinical psychologists for further assistance, if necessary. Learning disability specialists, pediatricians, neurologists, eye-care specialists, speech and hearing professionals are also part of the potential team to be of assistance.

You may be wondering why rewards do not work. Well, they may work over the short run, but not in the long run. Dr. Dornbush believes that promising a car or other ''mega-reward'' focuses the youngster's efforts on the importance of the reward and not on learning.

Keeping the focus on the intrinsic motive, learning, is what you ought to aim for. ''Do you need more time, books, information, tutoring?'' This question will go further and provide more long-range benefit than will short-range rewards like more telephone time.

Of course nothing works all of the time. But, at least according to the Stanford research, the more positive the approach, the more positive the grades.

"I Hate Camp . . . Take Me Home!"

If your children are like thousands of others, that summertime message has come across to you loud and clear. Maybe you've heard it on the telephone each night through screams and tears. Maybe you've read it in letters stained with tears (or some other human fluid which suggests that your children are being tortured). Inevitably, the message you get is guilt!

It seems that children typically begin their camp experience by hating it, but then are struck by the sudden realization of how great it is after all. Of course, this sudden realization usually occurs in October.

I, too, faced the "I hate camp" syndrome during a recent summer. When asked, "How can you do this to me?" I began wondering what in the world I really was doing to our son. He called to tell us that if we didn't take him home immediately, he was certain that he would become ill. In fact, he did develop a fever, and we knew we were facing the syndrome head on.

Homesickness, problems making friends, fear, traumatic situations at camp, or home problems all go into the "I hate it" syndrome. The most common cause of "take me home" among healthy children is homesickness. Do they really love us that much? Or, have we simply made it "too good" at home for them?

One couple I spoke with told me that their son ran away from camp so many times that they stopped sewing name tapes into his clothing and instead sewed in road maps.

So how do you handle the homesickness problem? Well, first of all the least effective and most potentially harmful reaction is to drive back to camp after the first phone call or letter and take your child home. You may be "telling" the child that you know she cannot handle it and setting her on a course in which running away from problems is reinforced.

If at all possible, stall for time. Suggest that you will talk to the child again in several days and see how well he is doing. Emphasize what the child likes about camp and remind the youngster how much he was looking forward to camp in the first place.

One anxious mother told me that she was completely perplexed by her child's sudden change of feelings. "I had no trouble sending Danny off to camp this year; after all, the T.V. set was broken!"

Emphasize that you have complete confidence in your child's ability to handle it and that you feel certain she will get over feelings of homesickness. Highlight how proud you are of the fact that she has found some friends in camp. You certainly do not want to underscore how much you miss your child. It seems that only makes things worse. You also would be wise to be careful about what your other children tell the camper who is away from home. If they are telling the homesick camper how wonderful home is, that's not going to help the situation.

Demands to come home once the dust has settled and your child seems to be enjoying camp, should be looked at in a different manner. Has something happened at the camp which merits further attention on your part? Is your youngster not making friends? Or has some other traumatic situation occurred? These do deserve your careful attention, especially if everything was going along okay.

Talk with the camp director and camp counselor to get a feeling for what's occurring. Suggest to them that your youngster's interests may not be being met. Also discuss what adjustment in camp programming can be made to assist your youngster.

What if everything fails and you do decide to take your child home early? First be sure that your child has given himself every opportunity to utilize his abilities to cope. The stress for your youngster may be too overwhelming. Children know best in these situations, so listen carefully. Don't force your child to cope with what for him is not "copable."

If you do take your child home early, be sure that you applaud the time she did stay in camp. Focus on the fun and enjoyment she did have from camp. Encourage her to be in contact with the friends made there. Don't let the early retrieval be a sign of your child's inability. Instead focus on what she did accomplish, the amount of time that she was able to stay, and turn what could be seen as a failure experience into successful coping — for however limited a time it may have been.

Finally, whenever your child does come home, be prepared to be amazed with five weeks of accumulated dirty laundry, even though he only went off to camp for two weeks!

Arguing in Front of the Children

"O.K., so I like to spend money," said the wife in the middle of an argument. "Name one other extravagance!"

It's an age-old problem. You and your spouse are having a disagreement. (All right, you are having a *fight*!) When it involves husband and wife, it's one thing. But when it involves your children as well, that's another. Now there is some recent research which points out some interesting findings on the impact of parental arguments on children's emotional health.

If you are expecting a clear-cut answer to the question of whether arguing in front of your children is traumatic or not, however, you may be a bit disappointed in this research finding.

It reminds me of the father who demanded, "I want an explanation and I want the truth." To which his son replied, "Well, make up your mind, Dad. You can't have both."

The research, which was reported in the *Journal of Developmental Psychology*, found that when long-term chronic anger is openly expressed, it may harm children — but not all children.

Young children may feel fear, while older children are more likely to feel guilt when they hear parents argue. One of the symptoms to watch for if you are in doubt, is your child imitating your behavior. That is, does he or she seem to show a great deal of anger? Or on the other hand, is your child overly timid, afraid of angry feelings?

Problems with playmates is an early warning sign that your marital arguments are spilling over and negatively impacting your children. Teachers describe these troubled youngsters as "frozen with fear" whenever the teacher shows signs of anger in the classroom.

Research has shown that these problems follow children into their adult years. One study of 100 single adults found that even as adults the subjects became upset when their parents argued.

While chronic open anger can have serious effects on your child's development, so can chronically *unexpressed* anger. This may lead to emotional constriction in your children as they begin developing relationships outside the family.

The key to healthy parental arguments, it seems, is the *atmosphere* in which such disagreements take place. If the family climate you have created is generally a positive one with emotional support readily available, it is quite unlikely that your children will be seriously impacted by your arguments.

Most couples do disagree from time to time — some more frequently than others. That's because no two people are always going to want the same thing at the same time. What is impressive is that most couples *resolve* their conflict and are generally able to contain their disagreements. Your children need to see the resolution of conflict to be exposed to all aspects of human relationships.

If you expose your children to only positive or only negative experiences, they will not be prepared to deal with the world as it really is. So don't be afraid to disagree in front of your children. Just be certain your home atmosphere is *generally* one that is filled with emotional support, if you want to minimize the impact of those disagreements.

And finally, don't forget to show your children the results of resolving conflict. Telling your youngsters you are no longer angry, or explaining the disagreement and how you resolved it, can be most helpful.

Caught in the Act?

Dear Dr. Mantell:
Now that our children are out of cribs and walk freely around our home, exploring everything in sight, an interesting situation has presented itself. I'm sure we are not the only couple to have this concern, so your other readers may find your answer helpful as well. What do we do if our children appear in our bedroom while my husband and I are making love?

Mrs. Y.

Your question is on the minds of many other parents. For some, it is just too embarrassing to talk about. Many parents — themselves raised to believe that sex is bad, evil, or dirty — react when interrupted by their children as if they were caught doing something very bad. This attitude is unfortunate, and one that would best be changed. A married couple making love to each other are not doing anything wrong.

It is awkward, of course, and may be embarrassing, but try to respond without guilt or anger. Your children may be frightened enough by their misperception of love making, without terrifying them even more by your emotional reaction to being ''caught.''

Some children mistakenly see love making as mommy and daddy hurting each other. Explain to your youngsters after you have been interrupted that you love each other very much; that when you two hold each other and kiss you may become very excited and enjoy being close to each other; and that you both were feeling very good and happy.

At a later time, it would be wise to set some rules about privacy in general and to allow all family members to have alone time when they want it, without anyone barging in.

Similar questions arise about nudity in the home. Again, many families are simply too embarrassed to ask about it. Generally speaking, as with many issues in child-rearing, a casual, natural, matter-of-fact attitude towards young children occasionally seeing their parents without clothes on can help to prevent your youngsters from developing a negative attitude towards their own bodies.

Parading around constantly in the nude, or having an ''open door policy'' even during lovemaking, can be overstimulating, confusing and much too provocative for youngsters to handle. That extreme is not healthy.

Parents who go to great lengths to prevent their children from *ever* seeing them without clothing may well be instilling an attitude in their youngsters that is not conducive to emotional maturity. Children may become so concerned with what is being hidden from them that nakedness and sexuality take on an unhealthy focus in their lives.

It is perfectly normal and natural for children to develop a curiosity about sex and adult bodies. They'll also go through times when they become quite modest. Again, treat the situation matter-of-factly, and honor their requests for privacy as appropriate.

By the way, you did not ask about the reverse situation, that is, ''catching'' your children ''playing doctor'' or exploring each other's genitals; not exactly the same thing, but a common enough parent experience.

There are three "don'ts":

• Don't overreact by being harshly punitive or strongly critical. It may backfire.

• Don't ignore the situation. The young "doctors" need to learn it is socially unacceptable.

• Don't get misled thinking, "It's so cute," that you become a spectator. (Don't laugh; I've heard many parents react this way!).

Do:

• In as casual a way as you can, simply suggest they put their clothes on and play something else.

• Let them know you think the "game" they are playing is not appropriate for them.

• As much as you can, distract them with another interest.

Now, despite all of this psychological wisdom, I ought to share my own son's reaction when my wife applied this approach. Several years ago she found Benjamin and a little girl friend of his both nude, having a grand old time "playing doctor" (or was it "sex therapist"?). When mom suggested she thought it would be better if they got dressed and went outside to play something different, Benj looked up and innocently said, "But mom, it feels so good, can't we hug just a little bit more?"

Of course it's humorous and cute. It also speaks to the point of children's fascination with sexuality and the human body. The two are not necessarily the same and it is important not to assume an early childhood interest in the body is bad. Handled casually, you can teach far-reaching positive lessons to your youngsters.

If the curiosity turns into an obsession with your child, speak with your pediatrician, who can help you determine how best to deal with it, and can help you decide if psychological care is necessary.

So, You're a Step-Parent!

Just being a parent in this day and age is a tough enough job. But if you are, or are becoming, a step-parent, you know that the job can be even tougher. To step in and help rear someone else's child is a difficult task.

The Association of Family and Conciliation Courts has published a pamphlet to help parents and their families effectively deal with the trials and tribulations that are often associated with being step-parents. I found their material very helpful in preparing these comments on the subject.

The questions that are commonly asked by step-parents include: "How much authority do I have over the children?" "How can I best deal with all of the feelings which arise in myself, my husband (or wife), and the children?" and, "What about the kid's natural parents?"

It has been estimated (1983) that there are somewhere between 25 million and 35 million step-parents in the United States alone, with the numbers growing each day from new divorces and subsequent remarriages. Fairy tales which portray the "wicked step-mothers" have not helped or made your job as a step-parent any easier. There's no doubt about it. Step-moms and step-dads have had bad press.

Fortunately, trends are changing. In families that I've worked with, I've seen step-parents who suffer not from a lack of love for the step-child, but instead because they care *too* much and want instant love and respect.

According to the Association of Family and Conciliation Courts, step-parents have three major choices: they can be "primary" parents, "other" parents, or "friends."

Primary step-parents usually live in the same household with the children. Their relationship with the children is like that of a natural parent, with the same sorts of responsibilities and benefits.

Other parents are probably the most widely seen category: they usually have the most difficult job because the children continue to have a regular relationship with both their natural parents. "Other" parents are often expected to perform many parental duties, but don't have the acceptance of authority that usually comes with being a natural parent. This requires long and sensitive discussions with your spouse, getting to know the children, and a lot of patience.

Step-parents who relate in a *friend* role most often don't live in the same household with the children. Usually step-parents who are "friends" have influence on their step-children more through a special relationship they develop with the children than by filling a parental role.

Here are some guidelines offered by the Association you may wish to follow to help make your job an easier one:

• First of all, *back off and slow down*. Children have loyalties to their biological parents which can be hidden at times. Respect these. You can't become a disciplinarian until the children let you. And they won't let you until they come to care about you. Care doesn't come easily either. If you attempt to compete with a child's memories of mother or father, you'll surely lose. Tell the child you don't intend to replace mom or dad. Let him know you can be a special friend and help him to grow up. Begin setting limits, firmly, after you've established your relationship. Most children will gladly accept you into their lives, and their hearts, if you haven't come crashing in.

• *Keep your marriage healthy*. Make sure that one parent does not always seem to side with the kids against the other. Be certain that you're providing time and space for the two of you to resolve disagreements and keep your marriage alive and growing.

• As a step-parent it is your special responsibility to *avoid making your spouse choose between you and the children*. He or she probably will feel plenty responsible to the children, maybe even feeling some guilt for the break-up of the former family relationship. According to the Association of Family and Conciliation Courts (and good common sense), those feelings need to be respected while you develop a relationship with the children in a way that is comfortable for your spouse as well.

• *Avoid competing with your spouse's "ex".* Respect the differences in the histories and the households of the children.

• *Money problems may present a difficulty.* An income which previously supported one household may now support two. The best remedy for avoiding money-related problems is clear and honest communication between you and your husband or wife and also, at times with the children.

• *Sexual matters must be handled sensitively.* The relationship you have with your new husband or wife may well be more physical than it was in your spouse's previous marriage. So be careful in attending to these differences and be sure you respond in an appropriate manner. It may be necessary, for example, to provide greater privacy for everyone, especially in the early months of your marriage.

• *Treat the children as unique individuals.* The "Brady Bunch," or "yours, mine, and ours" situation is seen quite frequently. Many step-parents strive for equality in the treatment of their respective children. This is totally unrealistic however. While equality is certainly a commendable goal, it is much more appropriate and realistic to deal with children as individuals.

• *Don't rush into adoption.* The question of whether or not to adopt a step-child should be approached with caution — and only after your present marriage is most stable. Before even talking with the other biological parent (if the biological parent is still alive), stability — and caution — are needed. If the other parent is opposed to the adoption, it may be wise to drop the issue, or to seek counseling in order to help find the best ways to approach it in a sensitive and realistic manner. A child more than five or six years old should share in the decision. If the youngster views the adoption as your attempt to eliminate or replace the biological parent, it is best to clarify your intentions. The Association of Family and Conciliation Courts indicates that it may be best not to proceed if the child remains genuinely opposed.

Keep in mind that there is no such thing as an ex-parent. Your new step-children will always have two natural parents, even if one of them happens to be deceased. Because they were first part of a natural family, they will continue to live with that influence — an influence which must be respected and treated kindly and gently.

Teenagers: An Owner's Guide

Alan was always a bright, shining example of what every parent wanted in a ten-year-old. He had friends, played in a number of different sports, had numerous hobbies, played the piano quite well and did well in school. He even began talking of going to college. Stanford, no less.

He was a good son, brother and grandson. He related well to the entire family and was never shy.

Until he turned 12-and-a-half. Then it happened. He became a... *teenager*.

He withdrew from the family, which he labeled "the enemy." Spending most of his time in his room, he began slipping in school and lost interest in his hobbies, piano and sports.

Alan's mother called. "We couldn't do anything right...it seemed as though we always fought. I was hurt and angry; he seemed depressed."

But was he? Perhaps. But very likely Alan may have been going through a variant of *normal adolescence*. Let's take a look at what that means.

My guess, that Alan's behavior picture was within range of normality, is based on a great deal more data than I've given you here. Typical teenagers go through the usual growing pains — finding out who they are; deciding if they like themselves (and often they don't); finding their own way; and adjusting to the many rapid changes in their bodies and minds.

What parent of a teen hasn't heard, "You don't understand me!" "Leave me alone!" "I hate you!" "I can't wait to get out of here!" These are tough on parents who, all too often, recall their own adolescence through a filter that washes away all of the confusion and anger, and allows them to remember only calm, loving moments. It is also tough on parents who may feel guilty enough because they feel they have "failed as parents."

I don't mean to imply that if your teen is in fact a more amenable, accepting, open and friendly young man or woman something is wrong. One recent survey of 1,300 teenagers found that 85 percent were "happy" most of the time.

The majority had no ill feelings toward their parents. But 20 percent reported "feeling empty emotionally, being confused most of the time." Interestingly, girls more often reported feeling lonely, sad and confused. More than 40 percent of the girls said they felt ugly and unattractive. Anxiety was a common feeling for both sexes.

Every stage of life carries with it certain tasks of emotional development. Adolescents, between ages 10 and 20, have the following tasks to accomplish: establish their own identity; give up childhood dependency; develop their own values (often based on their parents', though they are not likely to admit it); develop vocational goals; deal constructively with authority; learn to deal with the opposite sex; handle their rampant physical and emotional changes.

All this while — on the surface — "rejecting" their parents.

I say "on the surface" because recent research indicates teenagers learn to assimilate their *parents'* values more readily than they do their friends'! Sounds surprising, I know. Maybe also helpful. But the research indicates that the enduring values of the parents are in fact transmitted.

So, parents, let's take a look at what you can do to more positively influence your teenager, and get through the often tumultuous teen years:

• Don't fail their test of your love. Be loving. If you must withhold, withhold your approval, not your love.

• Don't insist on intimacy. Communication comes in many forms. If you're lucky enough to have an adolescent who shares his or her feelings, fine. If you don't, don't force it. Not that they will let you anyway. So help your teens find other adults with whom they are comfortable. Sometimes they'll find that person on their own; if *you* help, that person will be "tinged."

• Be sure your teenager has some reasonable amount of privacy. Believe it or not, you also are entitled to your share of privacy, and you can set an example for what you want by knocking before you enter an adolescent's room and respecting his need and desire for privacy.

• No matter how old the youngster is, from latency to adolescence, every child needs parental limits. It is her right. Perhaps you have seen the poster entitled, "If a child lives with..." If you, the parents are too permissive, the likelihood may be that your youngsters will interpret this as not caring, despite all their protestations when you do set firm controls. Make your standards and expectations very clear. At the same time, do not be excessive with your expectations or limit setting — this will only invite rebelliousness.

• Their problems may seem like little ones compared to yours, but it is important that you take their problems, no matter how small they may seem, quite seriously. This will show that you respect your child, which is something that he or she obviously desires. Communicate by thinking with them, problem-solving with them, and offering alternative ways of looking at problems. Do not ever expect them to take your advice and follow it.

• Finally, like everything else in life, adolescence also will pass. Keep your sense of humor and learn how to laugh at what is often only a temporary difficulty.

There are some indicators of genuine difficulty in an adolescent:

• Schoolwork becomes a significant problem.

• There is chronic and persistent fighting and arguing at home.

• There is significant difficulty in your child's social life, such that she begins to avoid friends and isolate from others.

• A sense that your teenager is "going nowhere" coupled with the youngster chronically complaining of being bored and "having nothing to do." This is especially noteworthy if the teen genuinely lacks any significant interests.

• Physical complaints, anxiety, or depression of a chronic nature (for more than several weeks). The physical complaints can take the form of headaches, sleep difficulties, appetite disturbances, gastrointestinal upset, and the like.

• Any self-destructive behavior, sexual promiscuity, drug use or abuse. Any mention of suicide should be taken seriously.

When professional help is recommended, more often than not I suggest a family-oriented therapy, which involves, to one degree or another, the entire family. While this is not always the case, and at times adolescents do need their own individual counseling, time spent working with the entire family can be particularly helpful to everyone involved.

Do You Know Where Your Teenagers Are?

Do you really care? Well if you do, imagine 75 teenagers who would be willing to let you follow them around for seven days to find out just what they are up to. Impossible? Not really.

That's just what a group of social scientists at the University of Chicago did in a recent study. They randomly selected 75 teens, ages 13 to 18, from among 4,000 students at a Chicago area high school.

Actually, they didn't quite follow them around. Instead — get this — they got the teenagers to wear "beepers." At random times for seven days during the hours of 7:30 A.M. to 10:30 P.M. (weekends to 1:30 A.M.), they activated the beeper, signalling the teenager to record his or her thoughts, feelings, and activities at the time.

Each subject was "beeped" randomly 49 times during the week. The researchers collected close to 3,000 responses over the course of a year. The self-reports were found to be very reliable.

At last we can paint a portrait of a "normal" teenager: what they do, with whom they spend time, what's on their minds, how they feel. The study is really ingenious. Sort of like being a little fly watching what your children do when you're not with them.

Now, what did these researchers find? Well first, a whopping 41 percent of the teens' lives were spent at home, 32 percent at school and 27 percent in "public" places — cars, buses, parks, on the streets or with their friends.

The largest amount of the teenagers' time (42 hours per week) was spent relaxing: socializing (46 percent), watching television (7.2 percent), nonschool reading (3.5 percent), sports and games (3.4 percent) and listening to music (1.4 percent).

Guess what the most prevalent activity was? Well, one-third of their day was spent talking with friends. Thirteen percent of that talking was on the telephone!

Now this may not come as a shock, but these normal kids spent only 4.8 percent of their time with one or both of their parents. In contrast, 29 percent of their time was spent with their friends. Twenty-five percent of their time was spent alone.

They devoted about one-quarter of their time to schooling. But, of the 20 hours or so a week they spent in classes, they reported only four hours spent listening to their teachers!

Loneliness was often described by these teens. But interestingly, those who had periods of solitude seemed to enjoy family and friends more. Mood swings were quite common, and lasted about one-half hour — 15 minutes in an up mood and 15 minutes in a low mood.

They also discovered this important finding: Teens who spent more time with their families and less with their peers reported higher grades, better school attendance and more favorable teacher ratings on scales of intellectual involvement.

Now, don't run out and purchase a little pocket pager for your teen. Chances are you'll get bopped instead of the teen getting beeped. But as you compare your son or daughter to these statistics, you may find what was so worrisome is only normal. For example, parents will bring a 14- or 15-year-old girl to my office because, "Dr., she's so moody and won't spend any time with us. All she does is live in her room or talk on the telephone!" Well, recall these statistics. Mood swings are a healthy part of adolescence. In fact, those teenagers who reported the most swings were as happy and in control as their peers.

If you want further information, I recommend reading *Being Adolescent: Conflict and Growth in the Teen-Age Years*. It isn't easy reading, but it is filled with all sorts of interesting findings.

Daddy Loved Me Too Much

Dear Dr. Mantell:
This is a very difficult letter for me to write because it means finally acknowledging what happened to me. I have been carrying around a burden in my mind for so many years, I just can't continue without bursting. You read so much today about child abuse and child molestation, and everyone talks about it, thinking it always happens to someone else. However, it did not happen to someone else. It happened to me.

Yes, even in an upper middle class family, growing up right here in San Diego more years ago than I care to remember, my father molested both me and my sister. She and I shared this with each other only when we became adults. The shame, secrecy, guilt and anger are more than any young girl should ever have to bear.

I would appreciate your thoughts on child molestation and incest so that others may benefit from knowing something more about what I think is an all-too-common experience.
Mrs. S.

Thank you very much for what, I am sure, must have been a very painful and difficult letter to write. Your experiences are in fact quite common, even to the point of not sharing it with a co-victim until years and years later.

While brother-sister incest is thought by many professionals to be most common, today we hear more about cases of parent-child — or adult-child — molestation than any other form.

You may not be aware, but the State of California, like many other states, requires psychologists and others in similar positions with the public to report cases of child abuse and sexual molestation, thereby protecting children who may be unable to come forward and discuss their experiences for a variety of fears.

I don't believe there is a psychologist around who would disagree with the statement that incest is a highly damaging psychological experience which oftentimes leads to a variety of other difficulties. Prostitution, suicide attempts, substance abuse, and some types of criminal behavior are common among adults who were victims, not to mention the possibility of having significant difficulties in male-female relationships . In fact, Masters and Johnson have noted that a variety of sexual problems show up years later in victims of sexual abuse. Difficulties in forming close relationships, allowing and encouraging intimacy with others, having trusting relationships, all are part and parcel of the aftermath of being victimized in this manner. I have seen far too many women who expect men to reject them, hurt them, punish them, and betray them, only to find out after psychotherapy has progressed for awhile that the woman was victimized by her own father, uncle or brother.

There are many estimates as to the number of children who are sexually abused each year by their parent or parent figures. One series of studies done in the late 1970's indicates that somewhere between fifty and seventy-five thousand children a year are victims of sexual abuse. Other estimates are much higher. Professionals generally estimate that at least one woman in five has experienced some form of sexual assault by the time she is 18. Most of these incidents occur in the family.

As with many sexual behaviors, there are a number of myths that surround incest. Incest, for example, is not restricted to poor, uneducated families. As you indicate in your letter, you were in an upper middle class family right here in San Diego. The incestuous father is typically not found to be "over-sexed" or otherwise a sexual degenerate. Despite the fact that we would not like to believe the numbers of claims made by children today, virtually all children who voluntarily report incest are likely to be true and accurate.

You did not discuss why you held silent for so many years, however, if you are like many victims of incest, you were probably made to feel that your mother and father's happiness, their love for you, and the stability of the family all rested on your willingness to participate in the incest and remain silent. Quite frankly, upon close examination, victims describe not only the negative feelings associated with this form of sexual displeasure, such as the pain, anger, and guilt, but also some have reported being confused by the fact that they feel satisfaction in being the father's "chosen one." This leads to very confusing, complex and ambiguous feelings in children who are not yet able to handle such complex thoughts and feelings.

What often begins as a kind of a playful activity between father and daughter such as kissing, wrestling, and touching, over time can develop into a gradual pattern of sexual abuse. At the same time, some report that incest begins rather quickly and it is forcefully done, especially where alcohol is involved. The patterns of incest, in other words, are as diverse as the families who are involved with it.

I mention "families" because incest is a family issue. This is a serious and significantly harmful act. However, the family system must be studied and treated when incest is caught early enough. One study found, rather dramatically, that in more than two-thirds of cases reported, even after incest is discovered by a mother she does not try to help or protect her child. In these cases, a mother may actually force her daughter into her role as victim, in this way having a buffer between herself and her husband. At the same time, many mothers are unable to stop it because of the fear of being hurt physically by the husband. Some also feel worried and anxious about the possible break-up of their family if the husband is put in jail. This is why so many mothers in these cases, often themselves the victims of sexual abuse as kids, are rather dependent people who frankly withdraw from their families through depression or other means of avoiding their husbands.

I have restricted my comments to parent-child incest because that is the most widely reported form, and the one you described in your letter. My concern is that you have been holding your feelings in for many years, and have not found it comfortable to share with anyone else until this time.

I recommend that you discuss your feelings with a trusted person — whether that be your husband, another family member, friend, physician, or a therapist. Coming to understand that you were not to blame and to be able to put into some healthier perspective what has happened to you is surely needed. The betrayal you have felt from your parents, the guilt and fear you have likely experienced, the confusion — all of this is more than any one person ought to deal with.

My recommendation is that you let some of this information come out into the light of day, thereby helping you to see it more clearly. Many professionals have had a great deal of experience in dealing with victims such as you and can handle this in a sensitive and caring manner. Find one, and get yourself some help, soon.

Adult Children and their Parents

No matter how old we get, we still feel as though we want to be children to our parents. But an almost inevitable shift occurs — often frightening, painful, and confusing — when we become our parents' parents. The change in roles is part of the so-called, "human dilemma." But it doesn't have to be a catastrophe — it can be a special time of mutual help and growth. It takes understanding, patience, caring and above all else, love.

From a parent's viewpoint, a child is a child forever and always. So in dealing with aging parents it's important to look at shifting responsibilities from that perspective.

One young woman in her mid-thirties recently told me, "No matter what I do, it seems my parents *always* treat me like I'm five years old." This same woman went on to describe her parents' increasing inability to care for themselves. Her mother was in her late 70's, her father in his early 80's. God bless them both!

Like many adults in their 30's and 40's, this woman could do well to acknowledge that while she dislikes being treated as a child, her parents likewise probably "hate" being cared for by their "baby."

Put yourself in the parents' place for a moment. You've led a full and complete life; you've done a fine job raising a family; you've succeeded in the business or professional world — and now, after more than a half a century, you feel helpless and dependent on the very child who has turned to you for help all his or her life.

The Yiddish saying comes to mind, "A mother can take care of ten children, but ten children can't take care of one mother." Maybe it's not that they *can't*, but that the role reversal is too awkward and painful to successfully handle.

Parents do *not* want to be treated as "has-beens" or *only* as "grandma" or "grandpa," generally speaking. So with young adults feeling disrespected and their parents also feeling disrespected, what's needed? Communication — adult to adult.

Stop shouting and listen to each other. Share your feelings about this life-changing event. Tell your parents, "whenever you tell me how to do something, I feel like you're not acknowledging my own adulthood. It's like you won't let me grow up." Tell your "children," "I know, because when you tell *me* how something should be done, I feel like you're ready to put me out to pasture and don't regard *my* adulthood. Stop patronizing me."

It's all right, even healthy, to say, "I really wish I were your little girl again and you *could* take care of me." If you create an open and supportive atmosphere of honest dialogue, you might hear through a sigh, "I only wish it were that way, too." Sad? Perhaps. But sad doesn't mean awful. It is, after all, a part of the agonizing human drama called life.

I said earlier it's important to *listen*. But it's also important to take care in how you *speak*. It might be fast to say to an aging parent, "You can't take care of yourself like you used to so I'll do it instead." Cruel. Why not instead identify what you're feeling? "This is difficult, but we are going to have to support each other now — you helping me and me helping you more than I have in the past. It's my life and your life. You've helped me make my own decisions when I could in the past and now I want to help you do the same." Self-respect is *always* critical no matter what age or physical-mental condition.

Treating parents like children makes no sense. Treating grown children like youngsters also makes no sense. Each is an adult. And each must be treated that way by the other.

It begins with solid communication. This can certainly feel scary if you've never had that sort of experience with a parent or child. But the agony of saying "good-bye," of separating, not only demands it. It deserves it.

The Graying of... Your Home?

After a recent talk I gave to a group, a couple came up to ask a personal question. Their concerns were very real and the sort many of us will inevitably face.

Their question? "What do we do with our aging parents? Loving them doesn't seem to be enough anymore."

Let's take a look at some facts. About 25 to 50 percent of people who live into their 70's, 80's and beyond will become dependent on someone else for their care. Of this group, only 5 to 10 percent will be cared for in nursing homes, while more than 90 percent will depend on their children or friends for assistance in day-to-day living.

There are a number of indicators to let you know when the elderly can no longer live independently. In addition to financial, social, and emotional issues, progressive immobilizing diseases (arthritis), prolonged convalescence, paralysis, and hearing or visual loss must also be considered. Memory loss, thinking disturbances, disorientation, emotional and physical outbursts are also signposts which demand attention.

For many senior citizen widows and widowers, the fear of being alone strikes terror in their hearts. No one should die alone.

Certainly, with some of these physical and emotional handicaps, many can live on their own. *If* they have regular contact with supportive and reassuring folks, family and friends, coupled with good medical care.

Beyond a certain point, it is just too *dangerous* to allow an aging person to be alone. There are tell-tale signs of incompetence: repeated falls, bedsores, incontinence, the inability to recognize familiar people, empty refrigerators, burnt towels near the stove.

After hearing all of this, the young couple asked me, "But how do we decide whether or not my folks should live with us?"

My answer was simple... tolerance. Especially from the woman of the house — who is more than likely the one who will spend most of the time and energy on the third-generation. This is not chauvinism. It's reality. I recognize it doesn't have to be that way, but in 90 percent of homes it seems it is.

Can you tolerate incontinence? Your children being told stories all about... *you*? Waking up in the middle of the night to change medical dressings? You must be willing to tolerate, accept and deal with these sometimes difficult negative factors.

Of course it's not all negative; there is often much good which comes from it. Elders enhance a family's life. How fortunate for a child to have her grandparents nearby! The grandparents are rejuvenated and the grandchildren have an enriching link to the past.

It is certainly worthwhile for your children to see you care for your parents. The love, compassion, and care they see you give becomes a part of them.

My wife's grandmother, Grandma Alice, has been staying with us for a brief while. My two children, six and four, are amazed at the delightful stories she shares. They are developing a sense of where they came from.

One morning my six-year-old accidentally bumped into Grandma Alice and she said, "Be careful, Benjamin, Grandma Alice is old and could fall if you do that again." Benj was amazed. He said, "I didn't know you *knew* you were old. I was afraid to tell you that."

He is learning something his parents alone could not teach him — and in a very sensitive and caring way.

The big question, of course, is "Should we put them in a nursing home?" One expert recently was quoted as saying that 10 percent of nursing home residents are in homes for inappropriate reasons. The overwhelming majority who are there have been appropriately placed. Despite the popular myth of children who quickly usher their parents into nursing homes, most people genuinely agonize over the decision. In fact, of those families I've counseled, many have placed strain on themselves — and their parents — far beyond what is reasonable while caring for the parents at home.

If you are considering a nursing home placement, by all means visit several. Talk to people whose parents live there. Walk through the kitchens, game rooms, and bedrooms. Speak with medical and social work staff. Take your parent for a visit, if possible.

The decision is a significant one and should be made carefully. Talk it over with your parent's physician for more guidance.

Does Your Family Need Help?

In almost all societies the family serves a number of key purposes for children, spouses and society itself. Through the marriage, the family serves as a stabilizing force in the lives of the adults. For children, the family contact provides a means for physical and emotional nurturance and healthy personality development. Society benefits from the structure of the family insofar as the group maintains and transmits society's culture.

Today, mental health professionals trained in family therapy view difficulties in more circular terms than linear, or cause-and-effect, terms. Thus, family members may provoke, maintain and reinforce one another's behaviors. For example, a daughter who feels unloved and insecure may act defiant and hostile. The mother responds with hostile criticism and rejection, increasing the child's feeling of insecurity, and provoking a continuation or increase in her symptomatic behavior. They may keep each other going in a repetitive, circular, never-ending pattern.

The child in this example is called the "identified patient" by a family therapist, but working with the youngster alone would ignore the interpersonal contacts and processes which must be addressed for positive change to occur. In family therapy terms, then, the whole family unit becomes the "patient."

Each family has as its structure what one family therapist calls, "the invisible set of functional demands that organizes the ways in which family members interact." Every family has its own style of communication. Famed family therapist Virginia Satir has described five common styles: placating, blaming, super-reasonable, irrelevant, and congruent.

One of the more destructive communication methods seen in families is called the "double-bind," which occurs when two conflicting messages are given, both leading to trouble for the receiver. A classic, often quoted example is: "Give your son two sweaters as a present. The first time he wears one of them, look at him sadly and say, 'the other one you didn't like?' " For the son there is no choice. If he wears one, it is no good and if he does not wear one, it is no good. Dan Greenberg, the writer/psychologist, has used this as a model for describing how parents inflict unresolvable guilt in their offpring.

Family therapists find it helpful to have a model of a "healthy" family. Let's look at some of the variables to consider in assessing the relative health of a family:

The family members must demonstrate trust and openness rather than oppositional attitudes and guarded, distant, or hostile behaviors. Respect for their own and others' ideas and perceptions ought to be shown. Power is shared and/or negotiated. Family members have a variety of problem-solving skills which are seen as flexible and adaptive. There is a reaching-out to each other and the community rather than isolation from the outside world.

There's a balance between clear, firm rules and flexibility when needed. You can tell each player without having to have a scorecard — parents are parents and children are children. Children cannot manipulate parents. Closeness and separateness are encouraged.

The family sees itself in a way that is congruent with how others see it. There is basically an atmosphere of warmth, affection, and caring. A high degree of spontaneity may be found with humor both acceptable and apparent. Sexuality is dealt with openly and comfortably. The passage of time is not denied and change becomes a part of life.

When is family therapy appropriate? My belief is that family therapy is almost always indicated when the youngster is the identified patient. Parent-adolescent conflicts, marital disharmony, and such life crises as the death of a family member are all strong indicators, in general, for family therapy. I often recommend family sessions for alcoholism, eating disorders and other such conditions where the individual symptom is intertwined with the marital and family dynamics.

Family therapy is not indicated with individuals who need help in separating from their parents. This may involve an adolescent or young adult who is too dependent on mother or father.

The late Dr. Nathan Ackerman, a pioneer of family therapy procedures, wrote that "troubled families are everywhere. Family relations are out of kilter. After an upset, the family seems less able to bounce back and regain its balance. It looks for all the world as though it is falling apart. Unlike Humpty-Dumpty, however, it may well pull itself together.''

In treatment, family therapists employ a variety of very interesting, innovative and creative strategies which typically allow active participation. Some use video tape and allow family members to view themselves in action. Thus, a mother may find herself saying, "I love you," but at the same time actually turning away or withdrawing from her child or husband. This family member then becomes confused, realizing that the words and the reality do not match. Another tactic involves the therapist asking one family member to arrange a family "sculpture" according to that individual's view of the family's relations. Some members may be positioned close together with others set off at a distance. The therapist, then, can perceive how each family member sees the others.

One of the most common questions that parents ask is: "When do we exclude the children from the sessions?" When specific areas of concern to the adults — such as financial, sexual, or family management issues — come up, then the younger members of the family may be excluded. The statement given to the children, that mother and father have boundaries around their relationship and are unified as a team in managing the family, is a healthy one. At times an individual may need attention aside from the family, such as when a father may be chronically distant and apart from his wife and children. He may need to explore some unresolved pain from his own childhood before becoming more emotionally available.

One case involving a family of a ten-year-old youngster who refused to go to school and was a behavior problem at home, reveals quite well the dynamics of a family treatment. When the family was brought together an inter-generational conflict emerged. That is, it was discovered that whenever the parents were arguing the youngster got himself into trouble and drew their anger off one another onto himself. Quite naturally this, in turn, created more tension and stress in the home. When the therapist directed the discussion to the issue of why the parents were constantly fighting, it became clear that the husband felt neglected because his wife was quite attached to her mother. Thus, the youngster's difficulties at home and at school were in reaction to another problem that was, as indicated earlier, a multi-generational one.

Finding the causes, and making changes in troubled relationships, are basically what family therapy is about.

Part 4.

Your Health

You're rummaging through the antique store in your neighborhood and you find a beautiful copper lantern. Of course, you don't believe in magic, but you rub the side of the lantern anyway. Suddenly, smoke pours from the spout and transforms into a giant genie, who smiles down on you. In a deep, menacing voice he informs you that you have one wish, and you'd better make it a good one.

You close your eyes, rub your chin and think as hard as you can. Possibilities flicker past: wealth, wisdom, beauty. Finally, it strikes you. "Health," you say. "I want good health!"

The genie's eyes widen. He nods assent. Obviously you've made a wise and judicious choice. Then he pauses. He furrows his brow in contemplation. Something's wrong. At last, he pushes his face close to yours and asks, "Mental health or physical health?"

It's a tough choice. The two are so interdependent that often they can't be separated. Chances are we're not King Solomons. Yet every day we make choices that impact one or the other. The results of these decisions can dramatically improve or diminish the way we live.

Sometimes we do damage to ourselves in our attempts to cope with stress. We even say to ourselves that we're doing harmful things because we want to. People still smoke, for example, even though they know that smoking destroys health. Alcoholism and drug abuse may go untreated. Diseases such as bulimia are kept under wraps while the person endures mental anguish and physical damage.

Teen peer pressure, the drive to succeed, the fear of failure, the need for love, the absence of it. These things steer us through our days and lead us, at times, into unhappy and unhealthy places.

You *can* take control of the wheel. Look up at that genie and say, "I want it all and I can have it!" A young woman told me the only thing her grandmother wished for her was "good health." Without it, the grandmother said, you have nothing.

The following chapters discuss such topics as smoking, drug abuse, alcoholism, bulimia, hypochondria, phobias and impotence. My goal is to provide some insight into mental health and offer some suggestions to help you improve and maintain your health in general.

Bare Your Soul – Build Your Body

Are you ready for the latest fitness craze? No, it's not Jazzercise, aerobic dancing, Splashdance, or Trimnastics. It may be as painful — in fact, it may be *more* painful. But, as they say, "No pain...no gain."

So what is this new health trip? I know you'll shake your head, but here it is anyway.

Confession. Yes, confiding in others about your troubles and traumas has been shown to have some actual long-term health benefits. This, according to some fascinating research at Harvard University and Southern Methodist University.

This is for real, so stop smirking. The study, reported in the *Journal of Abnormal Psychology*, was conducted by James Pennebaker, a leading research scientist in the field of behavioral medicine.

Let's take a look at this new body-building kick that requires no expensive warm-up suits, running shoes, or exercise equipment. It does require a very trusting person — who may be far more difficult to find than the newest "Fila" or "Ellesse" outfit.

The research on confiding points to the belief that when you speak your unspoken remorse, or share your onerous emotional burdens, your body appears to be less vulnerable to illness. Harvard's studies have found that the immune system is less effective in people who are unable to share life's troubling intimacies.

Holding it all in — when you are afraid to share your feelings, your problems and your hurts — requires a special effort. It goes against the natural flow. Like a dam that blocks the river, the more you have to dam up, the more pressure on the wall. Eventually it needs more and more reinforcement or it will come crashing down. The pressure cooker needs a safety valve. So do you.

This may help to explain why bereavement is a time so often associated with physical ailments, accidents, even suicide, for the survivors. Research shows us that when you keep your grief to yourself, you are more likely to experience health problems. When you are willing to confide in others, the likelihood of health difficulties decreases. Every year eight million Americans suffer the death of a close family member. Survivors with strong social supports and people in whom they can confide suffer fewer health problems.

Confession and pardon have deep roots in our theological traditions. In Leviticus (Lev. 23: 26-32), we are told that we shall "afflict our souls." In the "Al Het," Jews confess, ask for forgiveness, pardon and atonement. Confessing sins to a priest is an integral part of Roman Catholic religious practice.

It is interesting to note that confiding can be as effective in promoting health when it is *written* as when it is spoken. One group studied, who wrote about personal traumas for four 15-minute periods over consecutive nights, made fewer visits to doctors for a six-month period than did other volunteers who only wrote about trivial thoughts.

This may sound a bit weak to some of you skeptics. Those of you who belong to "Exercisers Anonymous" (you know, whenever the urge to exercise comes over you, you call a group member and he talks you out of it) take heed. It may not be painless, but the research can't be ignored. Confiding, sharing — getting things off your chest that you've been afraid to talk about — is good medicine.

So confiding not only builds your soul, but also your body. As you mentally review the "duties unperformed, the promptings disobeyed, the beckonings ignored," you are not just filling yourself with soul food, but with health food! I'm always impressed by the wisdom — the psychological wisdom — of our religious leaders. Thousands of years ago they developed one of the first health programs. And I bet some said it would never last.

Now for *my* confession. You see, it was when I was in Paris. There were these two blondes and...er, uh,.... Just kidding, Paula! (Maybe confiding isn't *always* good for your health.)

Stretching More Means Kvetching Less

This chapter will not be one of my meatier ones. It probably won't even give you a whole lot to chew over. Or digest. And it certainly isn't intended to give you much food for thought.

The chapter isn't written for everyone. Just the 80 plus million of you who are dizzy from all the diets you've been on. Those of you who share the same dream: to be thin.

Diet clinics, absurd short-term trips to the so-called "fat-farm" (absurd because you usually put the weight right back on), diet pills, weight clubs, diet drinks, diet books, staples in your ears, needles in your nose, outrageous food plans. Where will this all end? You've done it all, and you're still measuring time by the size of your body ("Last March I weighed 15 lbs. more than I do now — or was it 10 lbs. less?").

Being thin and trim is a matter of genetics, will-power, your environment, and your habits, perceptions and attitudes about food and eating. Mostly, it's about food — plain old-fashioned calories. For most people. So here is the "big secret." Are you ready? *The more you eat, the more you'll weigh*. Unless you exercise.

Now, most people don't plan to get fat, and most who are aren't happy about it. So what does it take to lose weight for the average person?

Quite directly, but not so simply, it takes major changes in your life-style. "Oh, is that all? You mean I can't just eat dietetic candies, drink dietetic sodas, and take grapefruit-garlic pills and shed those pounds? I thought if I just ate cottage cheese, I'd get rid of... cottage cheese!"

Sorry, but every piece of solid research I've ever read says it just isn't so simple. The key is not eating more diet foods. It is eating *less food*. And exercising more. And replacing negative habits, attitudes, behaviors and feelings with more positive ones. The key is behavior modification. Not the magic pill. For real lasting change, the only answer is... real change.

Here are some suggestions I've collected that can help you change your approach to food. Don't try using them all — that may drive you to drink. Do add several at a time to your daily routine.... See you at the gym!

• Put your fork down between bites.

• Divide your meal into two parts. Pause in the middle for a couple of minutes.

• Don't eat the whole thing. Leave some food on the plate. Forget the starving-children number your mother did on you. If there was a way to get the food from your plate to these children, you'd do it.

• *Exeunt omnibus.* Leave the table as soon as you finish eating.

• Don't drink a lot of liquids during a meal. Liquids move the food along faster and your tummy will feel empty sooner.

• Always eat all food in the same place. Stand-up routines are out; so is eating in the car, in bed or at your desk.

• Don't read, watch television or anything else while you eat. Concentrate on the flavors and textures in your mouth. Your goal is to learn to enjoy food.

• Eat out of dishes, not containers. It helps to use smaller utensils, plates, glasses and cups.

- Have someone else dispense the food. It's hard to fix meals for the family and not pick as you go along. Best: rotate the job.
- Make a weekly food plan and stick to it. Forget that the children should have a snack. If they must, have them make their own.
- Don't grocery shop on an empty stomach. And don't take along a lot of extra money.
- Eat at about the same time every day, including snacks.
- Don't leave food where it can tempt you. It's too easy to breeze through the kitchen and spot that jar of cookies.
- Plan your day around times when you will be hungry. Don't give up favorite eating times and foods.
- When eating in a restaurant or at a friend's home, don't be afraid to assert yourself. Ask that rolls and breads not be put on the table, or not near you. Be honest with your friends about what you are trying to do so they don't think you are trying to spoil the party.
- When in doubt, throw it out. Don't keep leftovers. They'll end up in your mouth.
- Re-route yourself. If there's a vending machine in the office, or a restaurant or grocery store that makes you salivate every time you pass it, take a different route.
- Zero in on foods that slow your eating. Hot foods, very spicy foods and those which require a lot of chewing will leave you with a greater feeling of satisfaction.
- Do some type of exercise every day to burn up those calories.
- Don't give up! Realize that you are going to slip up from time to time. When you do, forgive yourself and forget it.

𝕰at 𝖄our 𝕳eart 𝐎ut

There are telltale little signs that warn you when you're gaining weight: Is your appendix scar now fourteen inches wide? Did the dimple you thought you had on your knee turn out to be your belly button?

In order to avoid self-defeating behavior you must avoid negative thinking. You can identify your thinking as faulty: if you base your actions and moods on beliefs or fallacies rather than on facts; if you generally think in either/or terms; if you find yourself emphasizing what's wrong instead of what's right with you; and if your focus is on the obstacles of life instead of the opportunities.

These concepts are based on the work of Dr. Richard B. Stuart, and are described in his famous book *Act Thin Stay Thin*. Stuart also points out you are a faulty thinker if you "expect results before actions and if you do not move from a knowledge of where you are to where you want to be in a series of *small* and *positive* steps."

• Try this for a couple of days: write down the words you use when you think about yourself and your life at stressful moments. Now try to substitute more rational, positive and realistic words. Writing it down makes a major difference, so if you're serious about weight loss and want to be as successful about it as you can be, don't do it in your head. Put it on paper.

Think about the most negative things you tell yourself. What are the two or three most negative statements you have about yourself that you say in your head every day? Write them down. Then re-read them and change them into positive self-statements.

So, "I was born to be fat" can be changed into "Thin is a set of behaviors that has already begun to develop." "I'll never lose weight" can become "Of course I will lose some weight!"

Rewrite them in positive ways and plan to repeat these positive self-statements at regular times every day. Decide *in advance* the times and situations when you will use your new positive messages.

By doing this you begin to change your chances of accomplishing your behavior change objectives. If you think of yourself as weak and fat, you will continue to engage in weak, fat behavior. By changing your thoughts about your body image and self-control at regular times, you increase the chances of reaching your goals.

• You must also build your resistance to food and food advertisements. Brace yourself, but did you know that back in 1975, from January to September, there were 8166 cereal commercials, 4083 ads for candy, 3208 ads for shortening and cooking oil, 3024 soft drink commercials and 2,129 cookie and cracker ads on television? Of course you did.

• When shopping, you have to break the chain at the earliest possible point and have an escape plan if avoidance doesn't work:

...Avoid the ads.

...Resist giving in to demands from other family members to buy junk.

...Shop only when full.

...Steer clear of the traps set by packages and market managers...those beautiful displays that shout, ''Buy me, eat me!''

...Walk quickly, not slowly when you shop.

...Walk only through aisles that have food on your list.

...Shop with a friend and cross-examine each other, ''Is this really necessary?''

• Arrange your living environment to limit your accessibility to problem foods.

• Develop activities that serve as distractors to draw your attention away from food. Do this by listing the activities you now enjoy, things you enjoy doing but don't have the time to do, and things you would like to begin to do. Use one activity during the times you most normally feel strong urges to eat. You must be willing to do these things:

...Bring all food from your home, car and work into your kitchen.

...Eat only in specified places.

...Disassociate all other activities while eating except for socializing with family or friends.

This will help make eating a "pure experience." Develop an "Urge to Eat Self-Monitoring Chart." On the left side list the hours of the day. Label the next column "Level of Urge to Eat." The urge to eat level should be rated from "0" (no urge) to "4" (strong urge). Next, rate a "Y" or a "N" to determine whether or not you ate.

• Adopt a program of steps toward learning a "lean eating pattern." For example, wait two minutes before eating while you plan your slower eating pace. Place your utensils on the table between mouthfuls. Chew your food very slowly. Cut food into small, bite-sized portions. Join in conversation after you have chewed a bite, before picking up the next forkful. Make sure you are the last person to start eating each new course.

• Choose times to eat and stick with the choices. Your thoughts will turn to food, after a few weeks, at the preplanned hours only, because you have programmed yourself to do so.

Of course, these ideas are not new, nor are they complete. You must learn to manage your appetite during the day and night, control your moods (which underlie your urge to eat), get support from your family members, head off binges before they begin, and maintain your new weight once you've achieved your loss goals.

As you progress, think realistically, eat less, and exercise more. Act thin and you'll get thin. And whatever you do, realize healthy weight loss takes time, patience and consistent effort. Don't be like the patient I recently spoke with who told me he "doesn't lose weight because he's too efficient." I asked him, "too efficient? What do you mean?" He went on a two-week diet he told me, and finished it in three days.

Dieting Daily? Watch Out for Eating Disorders!

"Normal dieting" may be a contributing factor to the large increase in eating disorders and emotional disorders, according to psychologist Janet Polivy, Ph.D., of the University of Toronto. Anorexia nervosa, bulimia, and other forms of eating disorders — including obesity — will continue to be difficult to treat "as long as women are induced to strive toward a condition of ruddy-cheeked emaciation," says Polivy. "Only when society recognizes and agrees to treat its eating disorders, as it is now gradually treating its smoking disorders, will society's members be more amenable to individual therapy as well."

The psychologist and her University of Toronto colleague, C. Peter Herman, reviewed a significant amount of psychological research on eating disorders and dieting in an article in the *Journal of Consulting and Clinical Psychology*. Their review highlighted studies which demonstrate that chronic dieting is not only condoned but encouraged, especially for adolescent girls and young women. For example, in a 1977 study 77 percent of college women had dieted in an attempt to control their weight. Numerous researchers consistently link the "intensified quest for a slim physique and the dieting that such a quest seems to require" to increases in both anorexia nervosa and bulimia. However, the precise relationship between chronic daily dieting and clinical eating disorders remains unclear.

Although daily chronic dieting is now quite the norm, it generally requires behaviors and attitudes that may be seen as self-destructive and pathological, according to experts in the field. Daily dieters are often seriously dissatisfied with their body image and may be found to have very low self-esteem. These dieters may also come to think of themselves as failures, since their continued efforts to lose weight are often so unsuccessful. In fact, Dr. Polivy indicates, *"there is no evidence that dieting leads to sustained weight loss."* She further asserts that many people are able to lose weight only after going off their diets.

Classical research in obesity has shown that non-dieters frequently rely on cues from their bodies to tell them when they are hungry and when they should stop eating. Obese people tend to rely more on cues from external sources such as the clock, the smell of the pizza, and what other people around them are doing. Therefore while dieters may generally eat less than non-dieters under normal conditions, when faced by large restaurant portions, social pressures to eat, or social gatherings where food is made extraordinarily attractive, dieters will eat considerably more than non-dieters. Of course, the net result is a failure to lose weight. Chronic dieters according to Dr. Polivy, "should be encouraged not to overeat but also not to diet." She notes recent research which demonstrates that unrestrained eating is in fact most likely to result from dieting. "Chronic dieters are not playing a losing game," the psychologist says, "they're playing a non-losing game."

Tragically, anorexia nervosa and bulimia seem to be on the increase in recent years especially among middle and upper class women ages 12 to 20. Social, environmental, and biological factors seem to be the critical ingredients.

"Bulimia" involves binge eating, to the tune of up to 55,000 calories per hour for some of its victims, followed by purging — self-inflicted diarrhea or vomiting to keep from retaining the enormous amounts of food eaten. It's a growing problem psychologically, socially, and medically. The number of patients entering psychotherapy and seeking medical care for bulimia and its opposite problem, Anorexia Nervosa (a condition brought on by virtual self-starvation) is becoming epidemic.

Bulimics are almost always women. Only about five percent are males. Its been estimated that 84 percent are college educated, and most come from the middle or upper socio-economic classes. They are usually seen as having very high standards, with low self-esteem. They commonly fear intimacy and are conflicted about their aggressive and passive roles. It's a trap between fear and need.

As a group, the bulimic patients I've treated are achievement-oriented perfectionists and quite obsessive. They are also almost universally depressed and carry an exaggerated fear of becoming too fat. It's interesting to note, however, that about 65 percent of bulimics are in fact close to their proper weight. They are the classic good girls under intense pressure to perform.

The "binge-purge" episode averages about 5,000 calories per binge, with some women consuming anywhere between 1,000 and 55,000 calories on the average of 11 times per week. The statistics of these patients are certainly staggering.

One bulimic said this, "I would start at the Burger King with the biggest burger that you could get and fries and a shake and eat that there and leave with a shake and stop at the donut place next door and get at least a dozen donuts and eat that on my way to the ice cream shop, at which time I would get two or three sundaes and a cone to eat on my way home. By the time I got home I might look in the refrigerator to see whatever else was in there. Then I would force myself to vomit. After I couldn't vomit anymore — after a day or two — I'd start another binge. Before I decided to get help, I was taking 20-30 laxatives per day to also inflict diarrhea.'' For this woman, binging was a method of anesthetizing herself — of not confronting her problems head on.

While bulimic patients purge afterwards, obese patients who go on a binge do not typically cause self-inflicted purging. They also do not eat as much during a binge as the bulimic.

Most women who suffer from the binge and purge syndrome get into it by chance. The 10-15 percent of college women who occasionally purge after binges don't necessarily go on to make it a habit — but for those who do, many wait an average of 5-6 years before seeking help. Secretive behavior is a hallmark of the syndrome.

Sheldon Z. Kramer, Ph.D., a specialist in eating disorders, notes in personal communication, ''bulimics come from families where members are overly involved with each other.'' Family members often express a great deal of conflict with no resolution achieved; these types of family interactions produce a great deal of stress within all family members. Bulimia can be viewed as a problem of growing up. Bulimics often have difficulties leaving home, and mothers of bulimics tend to reinforce their children's dependency on them. The fasting cycle, or purging, relates to the bulimic woman's self-loathing. Her sense of self-disgust is usually so high that she feels good and ''in control'' again — disciplined — when her life is narrowed to self-denial as, for example, during the purging cycle. It is her way of trying to achieve perfection.

If you suspect you are bulimic or know someone who is, get some professional help immediately. Therapy and medical attention are both necessary.

What does this mean for you if you are not bulimic but simply a chronic daily dieter? I suggest that you take a realistic look at your need to diet. Are you doing it because ''It's the thing to do?'' Or, do you need seriously to lose weight? If significant weight loss is necessary, and simple exercise and diet alone are not doing it, then perhaps you might want to consider one of the more medically controlled diets for people who need to lose a significant amount of weight, such as Optifast.

For some, daily dieting is more indicative of low self-esteem than high fat content. If that is the case, look *inside* of yourself for ways to build your self-esteem, rather than to constantly deprive yourself, adding further to low self-esteem. The link between low self-esteem, dieting, and the significant increase in eating disorders cannot be ignored.

Watching Your Life Go Up in Smoke

- Do you smoke more than 18 cigarettes a day?
- Does your brand of cigarettes contain 0.6 milligrams of nicotine or more?
- After you awake in the morning, do you smoke your first cigarette within 20 minutes?
- Are you quite bothered or upset if you run out of cigarettes or find yourself in a place where you can't smoke for a few hours?

If you answered "yes" to three or four of these questions, you are quite likely *addicted* to nicotine, according to Robert H. Shipley, Ph.D. of the Duke University Medical Center. Quitting for you is more complicated than if you answered "yes" to two or fewer questions. If you're in the latter group, you can probably quit "cold turkey," without first switching to brands with successively less nicotine, or even using the new and successful prescription nicotine gum.

I have found great effectiveness in assisting people in their desire to quit smoking by using a combination of approaches, including: relaxation/hypnosis; brand switching; "Nicorette" gum; cold-turkey quitting; enlisting allies; making cigarette substitutions; avoiding smoking temptations; and learning how to maintain your emotional balance while rebuffing smoking "come-ons." Systematic weight control while kicking the habit is also critically important.

Studies conducted for the National Institute on Drug Abuse in the late 1970's and other more current studies confirm what I see in those light-smoker patients I've treated: Target-date cold-turkey quitting produces much better success rates than gradually reducing the number of cigarettes you smoke each day or week.

Moderate to heavy smokers, addicted to nicotine, must be weaned off the nicotine first while still using a target-date quitting method. There are two highly effective ways to do this. The first is called *Nicotine-Fading*. Here, the future healthy person switches to brands of cigarettes containing progressively less nicotine. From a list of hundreds of cigarettes, arranged from those containing over 2.0 milligrams of nicotine down to those containing 0.2 milligrams, the patient is assisted in choosing lower nicotine brands each week as the targeted, pre-selected quit date approaches. Of course, the smoker is encouraged by a variety of means to avoid compensating for the lower nicotine brand by smoking more cigarettes. A gradual switching is prescribed, with 40 to 50 percent per week maximum allowed. Failure is assured if this is short-circuited. Lengthening the process also promotes failure.

The second process is the use of *Nicorette*, a nicotine-resin-complex chewing gum, the size of a "Chiclet." The manufacturers of this medicine note, "Nicorette increases the likelihood of smoking cessation among participants in behavior modification programs. As used in the context of this... behavior modification refers to supervised programs of education, counseling, and psychological support. The efficiency of Nicorette use without concomitant participation in a behavioral modification program has not been established.''

There are possible side effects of mild nicotine overdosing, which while generally not serious, can cause the chewer to give up the medicine before finding a proper dosage. Physician involvement and direction for the use of the gum is required.

Hypnosis, another very effective method, helps promote quitting by inducing a sense of calm that can minimize withdrawal symptoms while providing useful guidance on how to quit forever.

I find in-session hypnosis, coupled with a self-hypnosis tape I offer patients for home use, to be most beneficial. Ideally, listening to the 15-minute tape twice daily for the first week of abstinence is especially supportive.

A date must be set after the gradual nicotine weaning, when a cold-turkey procedure goes into effect. This is generally anywhere from one to four weeks down the road.

I often advise my quitting patients to reduce their caffeine consumption. This is because caffeine in coffee, tea and cola causes nervousness, and patients are tense enough during the cessation process!

There are, of course, many, many specific ways to stop. (You've probably tried a few already!) Consult your physician for direction. The following specific recommendations come from the U.S. Department of Health and Human Services. They are designed to help you initiate the ''quit smoking'' process. Try any or all. Then quit.

- ''Decide positively that you want to quit. Try to avoid negative thoughts about how difficult it might be.''
- ''Consider those close to you. By kicking the habit, you will be demonstrating your consideration of their feelings and concern for their health, as well as your own.''

- "Set a target date for quitting — perhaps a special day like your birthday, your anniversary, a holiday. If you smoke heavily at work, quit during your vacation. Make the date sacred, and don't let anything change it."
- "Ask your spouse or a friend to quit with you."
- "Change to a brand that's low in tar and nicotine a couple of weeks before your target."
- "Decide you will smoke only during odd or even hours of the day."
- "Decide beforehand how many cigarettes you'll smoke during the day. For each additional smoke, give a dollar to your favorite charity."
- "Stop buying cigarettes by the carton. Wait until one pack is empty before buying another."
- "Don't empty your ashtrays. This will not only remind you of how many cigarettes you have smoked each day, but the sight and smell of stale butts also will be very unpleasant."

So there you have a variety of smoke-ending strategies. Now some of you may try one, two or all of them and find success. Remember that in the commercial programs out today, 20-40 percent of people are successful at quitting for awhile — many of that number actually quit for good.

I also know that some of you will think, "I've tried those ideas and *they* don't work." Get smart. *You* make them work or *you* don't. It's up to you — not the particular method.

Be good to yourself and those you care about. Stop smoking — and help others to do the same. Good luck.

Alcoholism

Dear Dr. Mantell:
My husband and I have been married for almost 15 years —
and have been happily married for only six months. Despite
every doctor he has ever seen telling him he has a drinking
problem, he continues to refuse to see that he is an alcoholic.
Every aspect of our life seems to be run by my husband's
alcohol abuse. For your readers who think that alcoholism is
something restricted to the gutter, I hope any insight you can
provide in response to my note will help them see that
alcoholism can be found in judges' chambers, physicians'
dining rooms, and in some of the largest corporate
boardrooms in our country. My husband's disease has
destroyed one of our children and has all but ruined the rest of
our family life. Any comments you can make would certainly
be appreciated.

Mrs. B.

Dear Mrs. B.:

The hopelessness of your letter is overwhelming. You
sound as though you feel helpless and lost. It is a shame that
your husband to recognize what alcohol is doing to him and
his loved ones.

Let me begin to respond by offering some working
definitions related to drinking and its associated problems.
We all basically can agree on what a *non-drinker* is: someone
who does not drink at all, or who may have a drink on a special
occasion (eg. a toast at a wedding). A *social drinker* is one
who drinks more or less steadily, but at a predictable rate:
maybe a couple of drinks per week, up to one or two drinks
per day. An *alcohol abuser* is one who seriously abuses

alcohol on isolated occasions. This is not alcoholism as we know it formally, though this sort of person can certainly die of alcohol abuse (by causing a highway fatality, for example) just as easily as someone with alcoholism. *Alcoholics* are those whose continuous use of alcohol affects all major areas of their lives. After the first drink, alcoholics cannot predict their own behavior. Alcoholics consume alcohol in widely varying amounts at different times.

Your husband certainly is not alone. It is estimated that 70 percent of the United States population older than 15 drinks alcohol occasionally (social drinkers, abusers, and alcoholics), with more than five percent of the total population being alcoholics. Alcoholism has become a major health hazard for children as well.

The ten million or more alcoholics in our country are responsible for huge percentages of all hospital admissions, attempted suicides, broken marriages, traffic arrests, fatal automobile accidents and loss of employee productivity. The figures are staggering. Premature death (occurring from age 50 to 60, or perhaps earlier) is ten times more common for the alcoholic than for the non-alcoholic. Premature death can result from the complications of liver disease, injuries due to accidents, or even suicide.

Your letter bears testimony to the fact that alcoholism is a disease of denial. Recovering alcoholics refer to their rationalization as, "stinking thinking." Denial and rationalization make the disease of alcoholism difficult for the alcoholic to recognize, and make it difficult for the process of treatment to begin.

Here are some *behavioral symptoms* used to help diagnose alcoholism, listed in order from early to later signs:

- gulping instead of sipping alcohol;
- starting arguments with family while under the influence;
- friends commenting on changed personality;
- continuously drinking until the bottle is empty;

- borrowing money to buy alcohol;
- drinking alone or in hiding;
- two or more drunk driving violations;
- family threatening to break up;
- supervisor complaining about poor performance or attendance at work.

The *medical symptoms* include:
- elevated blood concentrations of liver enzymes;
- memory blackouts;
- impotence;
- anemia;
- engorged abdominal organs and large hemorrhoids;
- cirrhosis of the liver with signs of blood flow congestion;
- tingling sensations in the legs;
- flushed nose and palms;
- withering muscle tissues;
- central nervous system damage including tremors, anxiety, poor hand-to-eye coordination.

Because alcohol affects the brain, the link between denial and alcohol is one which your husband cannot see. Even when he is sober, you must understand that the alcoholic brain does not forget or, if it forgets, it denies the link between alcohol and its consequences.

It has been said that the best time to approach an alcoholic is when he is in a highly anxious state, since that is when he is hurting most. Some alcoholics call this time in their lives "bottoming-out."

In my work with alcoholics privately and in the corporate world, I have found that compromises generally do not work. Programs such as those of Alcoholics Anonymous and similar groups, along with professionally supervised education and training, physical fitness, group counseling, couple counseling, family therapy, individual therapy, and proper nutrition, all taken together comprise an appropriate and effective holistic approach to alcohol rehabilitation.

I understand your tremendous sense of hopelessness and helplessness, but want to reassure you that help *is* available. I urge you to seek help for yourself and your children through a local chapter of Al-Anon, the family support group sponsored by Alcoholics Anonymous. Your husband may then come along, but be prepared for the possibility that he will continue to be unwilling to see that he has a problem.

I appreciate your letter; it may encourage others to get help at a much earlier time, thereby preventing serious difficulties from developing.

𝓝ursing a 𝓢ham 𝓟ain?

It may surprise you to learn that approximately 30 to 60 percent of all visits to primary care physicians result in no serious medical disease being found. Further, 25 to 40 percent of all patients who are not actually hospitalized have no serious disease. Some of these folks are seeing their doctors because they have created such emotional turmoil for themselves that they have actually turned their distress into physical complaints. The extreme of that condition is a syndrome called *hypochondria*.

In a very real way, hypochondria is a serious emotional problem. It is generally defined as "a distorted or morbid preoccupation with one's health and one's body."

The health care field has only an acquaintance with hypochondria, compared to our knowledge about other disorders. For example, it is felt that more women than men suffer from it, but this is not certain.

It begins in the 20's, but appears to be more commonly seen in the 40-50 plus age bracket. While the relationship to social class is not clear, it seems to show up more in the lower social classes. It also seems to run in families, perhaps as a learned behavior or perhaps as a genetically-based syndrome.

It has been described as an emotional disorder, as a social and cultural problem, as a thinking disturbance, and as something that can occur in the deep recesses of one's "unconscious mind."

Some think hypochondriacs are easily diagnosed. "If they wake up feeling real well and call their doctors to find out what's wrong with them, then you have a pretty good idea that hypochondria may be the culprit."

There is a constellation of symptoms that are, in fact, seriously observed:

• Vague, ambiguous, disabling, physical complaints that are often similar to normal sensations most people ignore.

• Stomach, heart or respiratory pain are the complaints most common sypmtoms.

• Belief in the existence of a serious, undetected disease despite repeated reassurance, negative laboratory findings, and the fact that the symptoms do not get worse.

• Constant worry about contracting future disease.

• Alarm upon reading or hearing about an illness.

• Total absorption in the suffering.

• Talk about little other than their health.

• Physical symptoms in response to tension.

• Relentless pursuit of medical care.

• Negative comments about physicians, while continuing to seek medical attention.

Depression and anxiety can lower tolerance for pain and produce physical symptoms. Sometimes these underlie the hypochondria and require special emotional care.

It is important for primary medical caregivers to recognize that a long term relationship may be the most "care-a-tive" agent available for many hypochondriacs to reduce suffering and improve their lives. Care instead of cure may be the ultimate goal. Finding ways to minimize, ignore, tolerate and live with symptoms is the responsibility of the doctor in these cases.

If you live with a person suffering from this disorder, understand the individual needs to feel accepted and reassured of access to the doctor. The patient should *not* have to have physical symptoms to talk with the doctor. Such persons need to talk more about their "heartache" and less about their "cardiac pain." Don't try to *convince* the patient, "It's all in your head." It may not be. They do not want to hear that nothing is wrong, and don't want a clean bill of health. They do want a sympathetic or compassionate ear. Offer sensitivity and understanding.

Surviving Cancer

You dread hearing what your doctor has to say. The pain you have been experiencing has grown increasingly more severe. As he looks over your test results, a small voice inside of you screams out, "It's cancer!" Now you need not wonder any longer.

The doctor says he has some difficult news to give you. He confirms your worst fears. It is cancer.

You've heard some health professionals claim that different personality types are associated with different physical illnesses. You begin to wonder whether or not somehow it is your responsibility if your cancer spreads. Friends begin sharing articles with you about the latest study that shows if you laugh a great deal, you can "cure" your cancer. Others tell you that they read an article about group therapy helping to cure cancer.

In the meantime, your doctor prescribes a course of treatment that is a great deal more difficult than positive thinking, laughter, or some other social or psychological treatment.

Recent research challenges the idea that there is such a thing as a cancer-prone, diabetic, or arthritic personality. The authors found that emotional responses are not significant as causes or effects of any of the chronic physical illnesses in those that were studied.

And now a new study of several hundred patients with advanced cancer comes to light. This research shows "no evidence of social or psychological influences on... chances of survival, or the likelihood of relapse when a cancer is in remission."

The study is quite interesting. The authors looked at over 200 patients who had untreatable cancers of the pancreas, stomach, lung, colon, rectum, and other organs that were expected to cause death within a year. They then looked at another group of over 150 patients who had skin cancer or breast cancer that was in remission and that was not likely to be fatal in a short run.

The researchers asked the patients all sorts of questions about their social life, their marital history, their work history, their use of medication, their feelings of hopelessness, and other aspects of their emotional and social lives.

The patients' ratings for psychological and social adjustment were compared with survival time (in the group with fatal disease) and length of time before relapse (in the group with the less severe forms of cancer). The researchers found no correlation in either case.

Survival, according to the authors, "depended only on how fast the cancer was progressing and whether it had metastasized."

The researchers pointed out a fair amount of evidence for a relationship between psychological and social condition and physical health, however. One study that looked at over 7,000 adults over a nine-year stand found that people who lacked social and community ties had a mortality rate two to three times higher than those with more social contacts. What is even more impressive is that these results held even when corrections were made for socio-economic class, health practices, alcohol use, smoking, overweight and exercise. The most confident — if conservative — statement one can make, then, is that, psychological and social factors *might* be among the many factors which influence the onset of cancer, or outcome for cancer patients with more favorable diagnoses.

It is safe to conclude that once cancer has taken hold, the biology of the disease overrides everything. At least according to the authors of this study — originally published in June, 1985 in the *New England Journal of Medicine* — advanced cancer is not more likely to spread in unhappy people, and is not *cured* by a positive mental state or good relations with family and friends. This emotional burden should be taken off of people to help them understand that it is not necessarily their responsibility if their cancer spreads and death becomes imminent.

While it would be nice to be able to believe that we have that kind of control over our more serious illnesses, perhaps it is best to say that a positive attitude, keeping things in their proper perspective, and being as hopeful as one can be, may ease the way.

Emotional support, friendships, and good medical care are all important. Group counseling, individual supportive psychotherapy and other emotionally supportive measures help make tolerating serious illness an easier experience. *Positive thinking and hope are important and necessary in treating illness and disease, but are not curative in and of themselves.* Biology, genetics, chemistry and good medical care — and sometimes luck — play a heavy hand.

Not for Men Only

It knows no social or socioeconomic boundaries. Some estimate that half of the male population, at one time or another, has experienced occasional transient episodes. And yet it has been suggested that there is "no other medical condition as potentially frustrating, humiliating, and devastating."

Impotence. Erectile dysfunction. The inability to have or maintain an erection that is firm enough for intercourse.

Let's take a look at some of the facts and debunk some of the myths. First, we need to define some terms. If you have never been able to have intercourse, though you can attain good erections by masturbating or have spontaneous erections at other times, this is called *primary erectile dysfunction.*

Secondary erectile dysfunction is the term given if you have been able to have intercourse before the onset of this dysfunction. Of course, secondary impotence is far more common — some say about ten times more frequent than primary dysfunction — in the general population. It also has a generally more favorable prognosis for treatment.

Most men I've treated complained of partial erections, too flaccid to permit intercourse. Or the erection disappeared when intercourse was initiated. The pattern varies. For some, erections are maintained only in foreplay or oral sex, or only with certain women. Others can maintain erections only when clothed, or only when "in control" of the sexual encounter.

While it is well known that sexual excitement begins *above* your neck, erectile dysfunction may be due to physical as well as psychological factors.

Alcohol abuse and significant intoxication frequently lead to loss of erection and libido. Chronic use of street drugs, such as some sedatives, heroin, cocaine, amphetamines, anylnitrate, LSD and marijuana also contribute to impotence. Prescription drugs may also be related to loss of erectile ability. Drugs used in the treatment of hypertension or heart disorders, major tranquilizers, antidepressants, sleeping pills, antabuse, and antihistamines have been shown in some cases to be related to impotence.

Hormonal diseases — diabetes, thyroid abnormalities or pituitary or adrenal tumors — are often implicated in impotence, as are urologic problems such as urinary tract infections or Peyronies disease. Vascular diseases, neurologic diseases, liver or kidney failure, obesity, endocrinologic disorders — all can have an influence on erection.

Emotional factors often play a significant role. Depression, fears and phobias, performance anxiety, relationship conflicts, guilt and shame are often seen as psychological culprits which create or exacerbate impotence.

Negative thoughts and irrational views about sex and erectile dysfunction often make the problem worse. Psychiatrist David Burns, in his book, *Intimate Connections*, identifies some of the more common distorted thoughts held by men with erectile dysfunction, including *Shoulds* ("I must have an erection!"); *Mind-reading* ("She'll think less of me if I don't get an erection."); *Overgeneralization* ("If I fail once, I'll always fail."); *Fortune-telling* ("I'm going to fail again this time!"); *Personalization* ("It's up to me to make her happy."); *Magnification* ("It will be awful, terrible, a catastrophe if I don't have an erection."). I recommend Burns' book for anyone who wants to improve a relationship — in or out of the bedroom.

The fear of failure, the pressure of sexual demands, the inability to let go and abandon oneself to one's sexual feelings are all related to erectile dysfunction. "Will I perform successfully?" "Will I fail?" These questions alone can create enough performance anxiety to dampen sexual arousal and cause loss of erection.

A negative cycle begins with these sorts of thoughts. Fears of failure lead to "spectatoring" — watching and evaluating one's own sexual response. The result is that one becomes less involved in the sexual activity, which promotes distraction and loss of erection, thus increasing fears of performance. Sexual dysfunction can become easily established with this vicious cycle.

However, even in cases where fear of failure or other similar anxiety is not the major cause of impotence, it can occur as a *result* of erectile dysfunction.

The reactions of men to erectile dysfunction are varied. Frustration, humiliation, depression, marital discord, and hostility are only a few.

Treatment for impotence includes hormonal, behavioral, marital and cognitive-behavioral approaches. Treatment rests on the idea that anxiety is typically the chief target to diminish, and confidence the chief target to increase. Since 10 to 20 percent of cases of sexual dysfunction are organically based (physically caused), most cases come rapidly under control with psychological approaches. By enhancing the sexually stimulating factors and reducing anxiety, therapy is often off to an excellent beginning.

Non-demand pleasuring — non-genital touching and caressing — during the first week or so is a typical element of treatment. Fear of failure must also be dealt with early in the course of treatment, to dispel the myth that an erection, once lost, is gone forever.

Obsessive thoughts about impotence, the therapy or other aspects of the disorder need to be reduced. The idea is to "distract the distractor." Selfishness is permitted in order to enhance one's own sexuality.

Negative thoughts may gradually be erased by "talking back" or questioning the irrational beliefs and replacing them with more realistic, positive ones. Give yourself permission to enjoy sex, and do not allow thoughts which put you down because of erectile dysfunction.

While intercourse is often seen as the ultimate goal in the treatment procedure, it is not. The guilt, fear, stress, anger and hurt which often are a part of the disorder must be effectively dealt with before treatment appropriately terminates.

The same is true for interpersonal issues, such as poor communication or relationship conflict.

While psychological treatment may be effective as a primary intervention, often medical care and treatment is required. Consult your physician for a complete evaluation or referral to a trained therapist.

This chapter is only a very brief overview of one form of male sexual dysfunction. There are a number of other sexual problems which couples experience, including premature ejaculation and ejaculatory incompetence in men, and anorgasmia (no orgasm, not being interested in sex, not becoming sexually aroused), vaginismus (involuntary spasm of the outer third of the vagina in response to penetration) and dyspareunia (painful intercourse) in women. These are all emotionally painful and distressing, and also usually require professional assistance to overcome.

Booze, Boys and Girls

This should sober you up.

Maybe you're worrying about your teen-ager using marijuana, cocaine, "crystal," "shrooms," or a host of other illegal drugs. If alcohol is not on your list, it's time you learned something. In a recent survey across the country, approximately one-third of high school students who drank alcohol at all were considered to be "alcohol misusers" or "problem-drinkers." Alcohol is clearly the most widely used chemical agent among teen-agers today, and is the one most likely to get them into difficulties.

Consider this: alcohol is the leading factor in traffic accidents involving teen-agers. Although teens represent just 10 percent of licensed drivers, they are reported to account for 20 percent of traffic fatalities, the majority in some way or another involving alcohol.

Youngsters who abuse alcohol between the ages of 12 and 14, according to a recent article in the *Journal of the American Medical Association*, are likely to have later alcohol abuse or other drug problems. Another important finding in the study was that those teen-agers who *neither* smoke nor drink have virtual immunity to later drug abuse.

I am always shocked when I sit with a family in therapy and listen to the parents of a teen-ager tell me, "Thank God she's only drinking and not using marijuana."

Kids are drinking with more frequency and at a younger age than ever before, and today's teen-agers drink with one thing in mind — *to get drunk*. Law enforcement statistics attest to the fact that the arrest rate for people under 18 because of drunkenness has tripled in the last ten years.

A study at the University of Michigan found that kids follow their parents' drinking patterns unless the parents are either problem-drinkers or complete abstainers.

Interestingly, children whose parents completely and absolutely stay away from alcohol tend to develop drinking problems, because they have not learned how to drink in moderation. On the other side of the continuum, children of problem-drinkers tend to develop negative attitudes toward alcohol because they see the difficulties that alcohol can bring about.

A strong self-image is the best antibiotic a youngster can have against the deadly disease called "peer pressure." I believe developing a positive self-image is the best gift that a parent can give to a child — more important than a new car, a big inheritance, or a condo while your kids go to State.

I absolutely object to teen-age drinking parties. The parent who says, "Well, what should I do?" ought to look in the mirror and take the tough position. Set down the rule: *no drinking, no drugs*. Be willing to enforce that rule by whatever means necessary. Chaperone the party and rid your home of other kids who bring booze.

I cannot overstate the harm done to teen-agers by alcohol and other drugs. As a therapist who treats families with teenagers, I have seen far too many kids and families devastated by alcohol and drugs. There is no good reason for a teen-ager to use alcohol or narcotics.

If you cannot depend on your teen-agers to avoid alcohol when they're not in your home, then they need to stay either with you or under other responsible adult supervision.

Educate your children through discussion — not by lecturing them. Inform them of the effects of alcohol on their day-to-day work and on their driving. Teach them about the use of alcohol in moderation.

Set strict rules, be consistent and enforce them. Educate your children, don't lecture, and watch for any signs of trouble. These may include: withdrawal; poor frustration tolerance; secret meeting and telephone calls; a change in their eating and sleeping habits; physical evidence of alcohol (or drug) use; change in dress; an increase in borrowing money; and new friends your teen tries to keep away from you.

It is essential that you know where they are, who they are with, and what they are doing. To combat alcohol abuse among teen-agers you must continue to do this until you are confident that your teen has developed self-discipline and can enforce your rules on his/her own.

Professional help in the form of outpatient psychotherapy or residential treatment may be necessary if serious alcohol abuse has occurred.

The Bay Haven Chemical Dependency Program, a division of Bay Medical Center in Bay City, Michigan, has identified three phases of teen chemical dependency:

The *crucial phase* consists of a number of critically important warning signs: decrease of attention span, low frustration tolerance, difficulty in school, change in type of friends, changing appearance and personal hygiene, stopping normal extracurricular activities. In the crucial phase, you may see your teenager lose ordinary willpower, exhibit impaired thinking, indefinable fears, and a bunch of alibis.

The *chronic* phase of teenage chemical dependency includes: sleeping in class, inconsistent behavior, change in the quality of homework assignments (if any are done), poor interpersonal contact, decreased ability to stop chemical use, increased absenteeism from school and work, disciplinary problems at school or work. Increased association with a drug sub-culture, no interest in school, and perhaps dropping out of school, are indications of major problems.

At the bottom of the chronic phase, the teenager may at last admit complete defeat. Some teenagers may never do this until they are adults. (Some adults may never admit this either.) A great deal of luck, patience, wisdom, perhaps professional help (and even prayer!) may lead to a turning point.

After complete defeat is admitted comes an honest desire for help. This ushers in the third and final stage, the *rehabilitation phase.* Under professional care, the abuser and family will learn that chemical dependency is a disease, will be assisted in honest self-appraisal, and will begin treatment. A physical examination and psychological assessment are appropriate at this time. Group therapy will be initiated. Therapy should lead to greater awareness of others, more concern for the family, a desire for education, and renewed interest in vocational goals. The situation will be faced honestly, perhaps for the first time.

Continuing ongoing support and psychotherapy along with Alcoholics Anonymous (AA) or Narcotics Anonymous (NA) are imperative at this time, perhaps to continue for many years.

Symptoms of recovery include an onset of new hope, "right thinking," diminished fears of the future, an improvement in physical and psychological condition, desire to resume hobbies, increased self-confidence, and contentment and rewards for being sober.

Although this description takes only moments to read, the process may take months and perhaps even years to accomplish. Going from the early crucial phase, where you notice small changes in your teenager's behavior, to complete defeat admitted, to onset of new hope and an enlightened and interesting life with sobriety, takes many, many twists and turns. Shouting, screaming, or stripping your teenager of self-esteem are not likely to work. Patience, understanding, and professional assistance are critical.

Incidentally, the path of chemical dependency in your adolescent may be related to your own chemical dependency. If you have questions about yourself or are interested in joining an AA group, contact a psychologist or call a local AA chapter.

Teenage Drug Abuse

My problem appears to be a common one among my friends. I'm a mother of two teenage children. Like all mothers, I'm terrified that they may get involved in marijuana. One of the boys is always a behavior problem. Any suggestions?

First of all, your "problem" is in fact a very common one. I tell parents of adolescents I counsel to *expect* that their normal well-adjusted teenage son or daughter will probably at least *try* marijuana. Fifty percent of high school and college students do. After alcohol, marijuana is the next most widely abused drug. About 25 percent of all teenagers and college students are regular, social users of marijuana. And it's been estimated that about 10 percent are hard-core chronic abusers whose lives are fully organized around the drug.

The common question is "why?" Why does my son, who has everything and more, turn to such a thing? Why does my little princess lie to me about smoking pot when she has a beautiful family, a nice car, a wealthy boyfriend, and her room was just redecorated. Why can't she be happy without the drug?

Sound familiar?

Drug use, such as alcohol and marijuana, is related to a number of factors, according to adolescents I've treated:

• Kids drink today for one reason — quite simply to get drunk.

• "To search for pleasure," was the reason most cited by 20,000 teenagers recently surveyed when asked why they smoke marijuana.

• Some believe that life is so overwhelming, the future so bleak, parents such "pains in the neck," school so frustrating, sexual pressure so difficult to put up with, that drugs and *only* drugs can solve all of their problems.

• Drugs are also easy to get. Ask *any* — repeat, *any* — high school student and most junior high kids where to get marijuana. They can tell you. Private school or public school. Even religion school. Peer pressure is too difficult for some children.

• Finally, rebellion is often cited as a key reason — when the abuser is being honest. Numbers of adolescent girls in particular have told me, "What's the difference between my smoking grass and my mom living on Valium, diet pills and all the other stuff her 'caring' doctor gives her just to shut her up?" One study recently found that if a mother takes tranquilizers daily, her child is three times more likely to use drugs than those whose mothers are not tranquilizer users.

So what can you do if you suspect your teenage son or daughter is abusing drugs?

First, learn everything you can about drugs and their effects. Know what the real risks are. Also, know what the laws are.

You should also know the signs of, for example, marijuana abuse. These may include unusual changes in behavior: withdrawal, spending more time alone, emotional instability, poor school work, irritability. All these are clues that something is calling for your attention. Give it in a non-judgmental, supportive way.

The signs of marijuana use also may include rapid, loud talking; staring off into space; hysterical laughter; sleepiness. The youngster's pupils may be dilated and eyes reddened. Distorted perceptions are also common. There are other more subtle signs to watch for as well. All too often, unless you catch them in the act, you simply won't be sure.

Talk with your teenager about your concerns. Do not lose your self-control. It isn't the end of the world and it could be worse. Keep your emotions under control so you can *listen* to your child. The more you overreact the more distance you'll create. Some parents threaten to throw kids out; to "keep you in the house for a year," "take away all your records and tapes." I find these generally useless. They need your help and encouragement to find more rewarding sources of pleasure — not to be rejected by shouts and impotent threats.

Family stress increases the likelihood of drug abuse. So maintain or build a close family relationship. Peer group pressure becomes more difficult to withstand when the family base is not strong. This means not only good communication between parent and child, but between parents as well.

Do not tolerate drug use in your home. Do not give the inconsistent and absurd message, "If you must smoke it, do it at home." Taking away privileges for irresponsible behavior makes a great deal of sense — if it's done reasonably and it's consistently backed up.

If you're not getting a sense of success, get some professional help — not for the drug abuser alone, but for the family as well. The family needs the help along with the teenager.

Peer Pressure Deals Drugs

Once again, psychological research has developed a set of findings which support good old-fashioned common sense.

A recent report on, "a new psychological model of drug abuse," focuses on the pressure and influence of "peer clusters." The researchers found that *helping children and teenagers to "just say no" is not sufficient* to provide the ammunition kids need today to avoid drug use and abuse.

"In fact," says psychologist E.R. Oetting, "any treatment or prevention program that does not ultimately lead to changes in peer associations may be doomed to failure."

Dr. Oetting and psychologist Fred Beauvals, both of Colorado State University, published their findings in the *Journal of Counseling Psychology,* a scholarly publication of the American Psychological Association.

Now, as parents I am certain that you know the importance of learning about your children's and teenagers' friends. What if they don't let you? That's probably an ominous sign and an indicator which should encourage you to check further into their friends, become more involved in your children's social life and monitor their activities more intensely.

Parents need the support of other parents in doing this; organizing a communications network with the parents of your children's friends is an excellent idea. When parents communicate with each other about their youngsters' activities, that's one major step in helping children.

Exhorting adolescents to "just say no to drugs" is "not going to work," notes Dr. Beauvals, because such campaigns assume there is some outside force that corrupts "innocent" youths. For example, Dr. Beauvals finds fault with a television message showing pushers relentlessly prodding a youth on his way to school. In reality, he notes, "that youth has much more to say, and is typically an active participant in that process."

Environment and personality may conspire to encourage use of illegal drugs, but these factors only set the stage, according to Drs. Oetting and Beauvals. *The most important contributor to adolescent drug use is the influence of peers.* "Peers shape attitudes about drugs, provide drugs, provide the social contexts for drug use, and share ideas and beliefs that become the rationales for drug use," the researchers say. Nevertheless they caution that *every member* "of a peer cluster is seen as an active, participating agent in shaping the norms and behaviors of that cluster in deciding whether, when, and how to take drugs." Thus no teenage drug user may be properly viewed as an "unwitting victim."

Associations with peers accounted for more than half of the differences between students who did and did not use drugs, and the implications for treatment are important. "Counseling, therapy, or any other treatment of the individual for drug involvement is likely to be of limited value unless that treatment also involves changes in the youth's peer cluster." For example, counselors might use the move from junior high to high school or from high school to college to help shift a youth to drug-free peer clusters. The recent increase in peer counseling, in which young people help each other, also may be helpful. Such programs, the researchers note, often identify members of drug-using clusters and use them as agents for change within the group.

Programs which make use of peer counseling, with young people helping other young people, are most beneficial. Your involvement as a parent in your youngster's peer relations are critically important.

"The results show clearly that the attack on adolescent drug abuse cannot focus on drugs alone; it must include dealing with problems resulting from family disruption, poor school adjustment, religious identification, and most of all, it must focus on peer associations," the researchers say. "Prevention efforts should begin early," and aim at "influencing a teenager's choice of peers and developing strong sanctions against drug use in peer clusters."

So, if you are concerned about your teenager's substance abuse (and which responsible parent today is not?), look at your children's social lives. Certainly the "just say no" campaign is of use — particularly for very young children whose attitudes are just forming. Education and other preventive programs such as those offered in schools today may be of value, but *peer pressure seems to be the critical variable* to which all of us must pay a great deal of attention.

Teen Suicide

"Time passes by
Minute by minute, hour by hour
As I see myself die.
No one around to relieve my loneliness
No one around me who cares.
Each day that passes
I see nothing but conflicts.
No meaning to life,
Yet no meaning to death."

A seventeen-year-old high school student undergoing psychotherapy for depression began to express herself about her feelings with that poem.

Depression? Suicide? Teenagers? Somehow we just don't think of teens being depressed, do we? Moody, maybe. Uncontrollable, at times. But depressed? What do they have to be depressed or suicidal about? Read on.

First, let's review adolescence — a "shake-up physically, psychologically, emotionally and socially." According to a National Institute of Mental Health study, there are "pressures from within (hormonal changes, body changes, sexual desires), and without (from peers — need for heterosexual relations, social approval, acceptance; from parents — for maintenance of grades, restrictions on dress and behavior)."

Achieving their appropriate gender role, accepting their body image, gaining independence from parents, responsible sexuality, academic goals, occupational preparation, and establishing values relating to marriage and parenthood — all are psychological and social demands placed on the adolescent. It is a time to answer the question, "Who am I and where do I want to grow?"

Studies have identified six core factors in adolescent depression:

- *Lack of self-confidence*. Feelings of guilt, lack of energy, brooding and sadness.
- *Social abandonment*. Emptiness in life, death wishes, and social frustration.
- *Loss of interests*. Difficulty in interpersonal communication.
- *Sadness*. Weight change, grouchiness, frequent crying, and feelings of hopelessness.
- *Somatic symptoms*. Disturbed sleep and feelings of loneliness.
- *Acting out*. Desire to run away from home, aggressiveness, and lack of self-confidence.

Suicide ranks as one of three leading causes of death for teenagers, along with accidents and homicides. A National Institute of Mental Health study reported that there is "an increase in negative life events, self-undermining, and family stress and illness — especially mental illness — in young adults and teens experiencing depression and attempting suicide. There is also a decrease in family supportiveness and one's own ability to cope."

The investigators, Drs. Hirschfield and Blumenthal, also found that "those persons completing suicide are characterized as being more active, aggressive and impulsive than individuals experiencing depression or attempting suicide. There is a recurring and prevalent theme of confrontation over some life event (poor grades, truancy, antisocial behavior), with subsequent humiliation."

More females experience depression and attempt suicide than males. However, the "number of males succeeding at suicide is greater than that of females."

Why do kids kill themselves? Different theories emphasize the influence of past events on present and future behavior, the stress of adolescence, or sociological factors such as anomie, alienation, withdrawal and isolation. The cognitive theory stresses the meaning of death for the teen, while yet another view stresses biochemical correlates of suicide behavior.

Suffice it to say that many, if not most, suicide attempts are grounded in a combination of longstanding problems coupled with the impact of a recent critical event in the home, school or personal life of the teenager.

A narrowing of vision — looking at life through a pin-hole and not seeing other aspects of a problem — is quite typical in the depressed teen. Parents and friends feel inadequate in trying to get the teen to "cheer up" and see life's problems more hopefully. Others just can't seem to help the teen to widen his or her perspective of the world. And suddenly, the teen does begin to "cheer up" a bit. Parents and friends take a sigh of relief — falsely believing everything will be all right. It may, however, be the sign that the teen has finally discovered and settled on the "way out." It is common enough to hear family members say that just before the suicide attempt "he seemed to begin perking up."

This is a social problem which can become tragically personal. Parents of teens must take seriously any of the symptoms I've discussed. My seventeen-year-old client-poet summed it up well:

"Never any happiness
    Only hopelessness and helplessness.
Shall the day arrive soon
    Or shall I survive.
How can I live with a constant lie,
    For..., she must die."

Caring for the Dying

Although it is not a pleasant topic, it is one which every human must eventually face. Where shall we die?

More than 70 percent of the present population of the United States will die in hospitals or nursing homes, according to one study. When it comes to the statistics compiled for cancer deaths alone, the number increases to 85 percent. Death at home, except in cases of sudden illness or accident, has become a relatively unusual event. Indeed, to arrange home care for a terminally ill person tends to arouse suspicion and uneasiness in those outside the family.

We all like to think of ourselves as highly sensitive to friends and family who are ill — especially those who are terminally ill. Yet most of us are not aware of the primary needs of dying patients: freedom from pain and distressing symptoms of disease, a caring environment, expert care, assurance that they will not be abandoned, a sense of dignity and worth, care which emphasizes quality of life, opportunities to reflect upon the meaning of life. Family members and close friends who are aware of those needs can contribute much to the dying person's well being in the final weeks and months.

Will I die alone? Am I so repugnant that no one will visit me? These are the sorts of questions which dying patients often ask themselves. Associated with these concerns is the fear of being a burden upon family and friends.

Unfortunately, terminally ill patients are often left alone to die. Families can provide care and help to the end, however — patients need not be abandoned.

The terminally ill need time to reflect upon their past, to recall experiences of pleasure and satisfaction associated with life. Family members and friends are needed to help the patient reflect upon the past, and to share in the joys and sorrows of the patient's life.

Be supportive and encourage through active listening any discussion about how the family will survive. It is useful to reassure the patient that it is all right to air these concerns. Obviously no one can guarantee the future, though dying patients often feel a sense of continued responsibility to family. Although it may hurt, discussions about future finances, social planning and children's dreams need to be explored. Though the dying patient will not be there to see these plans acted upon, relevant concerns need to be expressed. By doing so, the patient can maintain a sense of self-worth, dignity, and relevance in your life.

Patients also fear the loss of control and increased dependence. Allowing the patient as much independence and control over his or her environment as possible will certainly help decrease the frustrations that are often associated with an impending death. Chores and responsibilities which were once so simple when one was healthy now become next to impossible as the disease process unfolds.

Another concept which must be understood by visiting family and friends is "reflected fear." By this I mean the fear that the dying patient sees in your eyes. Your own fears of mortality surface when you confront someone who is dying. And despite your desire to be uplifting, hopeful, and cheerful, all too often your eyes will give you away. When this happens it's more than likely that the dying patient's own fears will be heightened.

It is quite different to be *concerned* about the terminally ill friend or family member than to feel *fear* about them. By developing your skills in caretaking for the terminally ill patient, you will develop a sense of confidence which will allow you to act less fearfully and more out of concern.

Other fears and concerns associated with dying patients include fears of pain and mutilation, questions about the afterlife, and grief over loss of family and activities. Perhaps the greatest fear is loss of self.

An alternative to caring for terminally ill patients at home or in hospitals is hospice care. Although you may typically associate hospice care with a building of some sort, actually it is more than that — it is an attitude of care. The person and his or her needs are cared for together with members of the family. The focus is upon symptom relief and "quality of life issues." In other words, when a cure is judged by physicians to be no longer possible, then care is provided prior to, at the time of, and beyond death for those involved.

For further information on explaining death to children and understanding bereavement yourself as an adult, I have listed a few books in the References.

When Someone You Love Dies

A recent review of the most stressful events a family ever faces revealed that the "comings and goings" of people results in the highest amount of tension, anxiety and emotional turmoil. The single most stressful event was described as death of a spouse or close family member.

Despite this, it is *not* uncommon for families to be psychologically unprepared to deal with what is quite likely the single most unsettling event they will ever face. So let's take a look at the process of mourning when it's healthy and when it's not-so-healthy.

Grief is a process — not a state. Normal grief lasts from one to three or four months, with three observable "stages." First, there is *denial*, during which the grieving person has clear images of the person in a crowd or sharp, vivid dreams of the deceased. The second stage is characterized by *acceptance* of the death. This is usually accompanied by a sense of despair and depression. A sense of hopelessness, helplessness or feelings of worthlessness without the deceased are often seen at this time. Finally in the third stage of grief work comes *reorganization*. Adjustments are made by the survivor and "life goes on."

This sounds so neat, tidy and organized. The intense pain, the sense of wrenching loss, the utter despair that goes along with the death of a loved one can't adequately be described. If you've experienced it, you know it.

Far too often mourning isn't well-experienced. Pathological mourning is characterized by grieving that extends months beyond what is considered normal; a false sense of "everything is O.K. — I'm really fine"; suicidal thinking and behavior; over-reacting emotionally to someone else's trouble; and unaccountable sadness at a certain time of the year. The latter is usually seen at the time of the anniversary of the death.

Some families I've worked with display their delayed grief and pathological mourning in striking ways. Family members may develop the same symptoms belonging to the illness of the deceased. Others have an increase in psychosomatic symptoms. Still others delay their expression of feelings for years until they are the same age as the deceased was when he or she died — then it all comes out in disturbed ways. Some folks become crippled with guilt, feeling negligent and troubled over the "unfinished business" that is an inevitable part of life.

Milton Greenblatt, a noted researcher in the field of grief work has stated, "For the grieving spouse the acute behreavement may seem like the end of the world; but it is only the beginning of a long and difficult passage from a shocking, benumbing experience of loss, hard to believe, and sometimes totally denied, to a period of relative tolerance of pain, and, hopefully, in the favorable case, a new philosophical and emotional equilibrium." Dr. Greenblatt's wisdom has been of comfort to many going through this process.

While the full process for a widow or widower may take years, the time can often be filled with what one author described as "hell — depression, anger, bitterness, fear, inhibition of feelings, confusion, loss of initiative, increased dependency on others, and a host of other changes." Not to mention the hard practical problems to solve, the social difficulties and the dilemma of what to do when the overwhelming expression of support from friends comes to an end.

Children face death from an unusual perspective. From three to five years old death is a like a sleep. You die and come back. So it's not that children at this age are callous, it's just that their view doesn't allow the sense of permanence adults bring to death.

From five to nine years old children come to see death as closer to how adults see it. They still do not see it as something that will eventually occur to them, however. It is only by the time the child reaches nine or ten that death has the universality and permanence adults know it to have.

Children deserve the right to "belong" to the family's experience of grief and sorrow — as well as joy and happiness. Children should have a role in honoring the deceased along with the family. There is no sense in allowing children to be exposed to overwhelming, frightening and uncontrollable emotion, but many children can be helped to understand death better by attending funerals where some degree of protection against such displays can be provided them.

In explaining death, keep in mind there is no formula that is always correct. Many parents confuse and disturb children with their explanations. It's best to be honest and deal with the death in a reassuring, loving way. Life has stopped, the body is buried in a specific place, the person cannot return, we have memories to remember.

It's generally better to explain the actual immediate causes of death rather than to be philosophical or worse yet to lie ("Grandpa has gone to sleep," or "Grandma went on a trip"). Some children who have experienced the death of a close friend's parent become worried that his or her parent will also soon die. Assure the child that not many people die that young and reassure them about their future life — what arrangements would be made to continue their care and protection. At *no* time should children be *forced* to confront death or the rituals associated with it.

When asked about the *best* ritual to help children deal with death, a wise and motherly woman gave this piece of advice which, upon reflection, can apply to helping anyone who is grieving. She said simply, "Just take them into your arms and love them."

Living Past 100 Years

If you used to laugh at life but now have to rest a week just to giggle a little bit, this article may be for you. Everyone wants to be able to drink from the mythical fountain of youth. Everyone, that is, who is enjoying life here and wants more of it.

Of course, there are those folks who keep themselves utterly unhappy and completely miserable. Why they would want to live past 100 years is frankly beyond me, except possibly to perpetuate their misery.

But for those of you who are fortunate enough to maintain your happiness and allow yourselves to be satisfied with your life, what you read here may enable you to add years to your happy life.

In their book, *Stop Stress and Aging Now,* Drs. David Gardner and Grace Beatty have reviewed some interesting research on centenarians (people who live to at least 100 years).

Gardner and Beatty have summarized seven theories of aging. I won't go into detail here, but they described such diverse ideas as "limited cell division theory," "DNA repair theory," and "free radicals theory."

Free radicals theory? No, they were not talking about Abbie Hoffman and the Chicago Seven, but chemicals in the cells which have an extra charge or electron. I know — it's far too complicated for me also.

Scientists in this country and in the Soviet Union have looked at a variety of people from different societies who have lived to be 100 years or more. Here's what a number of research investigators over the last 20 years have found:

Most people who live beyond 100 years of age are "lacto-vegetarian." They means that they eat mostly vegetables, fruits, and grains, occasionally fish or poultry. (If you saw the *60 Minutes* television show that focused on the diseases and poisons found in many chickens, you might be careful about the poultry you eat!) Many centenarians also have a low calorie diet: 1800 and 2000 calories a day. Their diets are typically high in fiber, but low in protein and fat.

Their physical environment generally enables them to have pure food, air and water. They are typically not troubled by pollution.

Centenarians often participate in physical activity which includes a great deal of manual labor. They have an opportunity to do deep breathing from walking up hills, bending and lifting.

Interestingly, their genetic background is not sufficient to account for their living 30 to 40 or more years beyond the norm. Surprisingly, their parents lived only three to five years longer than average, according to these stress and aging experts. It is also fascinating to read that many centenarians smoke! Yes, I said they smoke, but a different sort of tobacco than most people in this country. Their tobacco is home-grown and includes no chemicals. They do not inhale, and usually do not smoke indoors. Their tobacco intake is also in moderation.

Although they drink only with meals — typically a homemade brew — they consume the equivalent of about 40 ounces of beer or about a half bottle of wine per day.

Gardner and Beatty's summary of 20 years of research shows that people who live past 100 *expect* to live a long time. And they are expected by others to continue to contribute to society.

People who live beyond 100 years of age and control money maintain their roles as heads of households. Another consistent finding is that they have strong religious convictions. They have a very high quality of life and are not obsessed with time or deadlines. I suspect we will not find too many "type A" or "stressed out" people living past 100 years of age.

The research also tells us that married people outlive unmarried people. Centenarians tend to be people with family, social and religious ties.

So what can we learn from this? Well, Gardner and Beatty make the following recommendations: "Learn to eat right, expand your social life, reduce stress, make a contribution to society, get physically fit, control your life, relax, avoid junk food, get away from pollution or learn how to protect yourself from it, and stay in love."

If this approach works for you and you do live past 100, when you celebrate your 120th birthday, please give me a call. Perhaps we can go out and celebrate together.

Part 5.

. . . And The Rest of Your Life

If anything stands third to death and taxes as a sure thing in life it is stress.

A high-powered woman executive once said to me, "What I really want is a permanent paid vacation." She was very serious. On another occasion, I encouraged a man who was suffering a great deal of job-related stress to spend a little more time with his family.

"Put your job aside for a while," I offered. "It might reduce your stress and you'll probably feel much better about your life."

"My job *is* my life," he answered.

The rest of world ambles somewhere between these two sentiments. It's not unusual for us to spend more time on the job than we do at home. Even if we don't go off every morning singing like the seven dwarfs, off we go all the same. The best we can do is enjoy our jobs and receive personal and monetary recognition.

But there are problems built into the work ethic. Fear of authority, feelings of inadequacy or lack of confidence may diminish productivity or even the ability to keep a job. A person once confided in me that, even though he was an acknowledged "good worker," every time his boss came into his area, he thought he was going to be fired. Those who have become unemployed may suffer "Pink-Slip Syndrome," accompanied by its heavy baggage of self-doubt and despair.

At the other end of the workbench, the drive to succeed and excel carries its own bundle of difficulties. Starting a business, for example, requires tremendous risks and extraordinary dedication.

I often hear from the typical workaholic, ''I can't trust anyone to do my work. No one knows this stuff like I do. I'm the backbone of this place. If I slack off, everything will crumble.'' Stress will quickly recognize this person as a great candidate for partnership, and stress carries all kinds of emotional and physiological trouble in its little bag.

Of course, in the land of milk and honey, we may receive terrific rewards for hard work. The bottom line is this: Hard work is great, but take your time away from work just as seriously. Balance work with play and relaxation.

Stress, of course, is not only a product of the workplace. We all face daily pressures from relationships, freeway traffic, financial concerns, keeping up, ...even the weather! Sometimes the strain is too much, and you panic. Or maybe the continuous stress keeps you in a constant state of anxiety. Guaranteed to be tough on your health.

The pieces in this section offer some ideas you might use to deal with stress, or otherwise make your life more pleasurable.

Speeding Through This Year Won't Get You to Next

Isn't it amazing how people say the same thing to each other each December? No, I don't mean "Happy Chanukah, Merry Christmas, Happy New Year," or "Season's Greetings." You don't have to listen very hard to hear, "Where has this year gone? I can't believe it's 19— already."

I hear these two sentences so frequently at the end of every year that I decided to give it some thought. Why do people wonder where the year has gone? Where *were* they? In some other year? It's as though the new year has been hiding, waiting to surprise them. Like they didn't know it was coming sometime after December.

Wondering where the past year has gone must mean that you feel it sped by you. A woman recently told me, "You know, it's funny, but I feel like I just got finished toasting last year. I blinked, it was summer vacation, and now already it's time to welcome in the new year." Whew, it's hard to believe she lived through the same 365 days everyone else did.

Why speed through the years like there's someplace you are hurrying to get to? We are *all* going to get to the same place. Thank you just the same, I'll take my time. If you want to cut in line in front of me, be my guest. There's plenty of room in the Home for the Terminally Still, so what's the rush?

Leo Rosten, in his wonderful book *The Joys of Yiddish* quotes a folk saying, "Your health comes first; you can hang yourself later." That philosophy serves a very useful purpose if you want to reduce stress and tension in your life in the coming year. It puts things in proper perspective, doesn't it?

Now if, on the other hand, you are bent on continuing the same pattern of speeding through your life, the following New Year's resolutions may fit you well:

- Your job comes first; personal considerations are secondary.
- Go to the office evenings, Saturdays, Sundays, and holidays.
- On evenings that you don't go to the office, take your briefcase home with you.
- Drive fast because you are late.
- Accept all invitations to meetings, banquets, committees.
- Don't eat a restful, relaxing meal; always plan a conference for your lunch hour.
- Regard fishing, golf, tennis, bowling, billiards, cards, exercise, gardening and reading as a waste of time and money.
- Believe it is a poor policy to take all the vacation allowed to you.
- Never delegate responsibility to others; carry the entire load yourself at all times.
- If your work calls for traveling, work all day and drive all night to keep the next morning's appointment.

There you have ten resolutions designed to make the next year speed by so fast you'll feel like you didn't live through it. Follow those resolutions, and you may not.

I must give credit where credit is due. These resolutions are not mine. They come straight from an advertisement I saw in *Orange Coast Magazine*. It was an ad for (are you ready for this?) the Harbor Lawn-Mount Olive Memorial Park-Mortuary in Costa Mesa, California.

And, (ready again?) the ad noted that the fine folks at "H.L.-M.O.M.P." published their "Ten Ways to an Early Grave" as a "public service." Ahem!

But the momentum is too strong, you say? You've been living your life according to these ten steps for so long, you'll never be able to stop? Don't worry. A heart attack or stroke is God's way of saying "Slow Down." And if you've suffered one of these but haven't changed your lifestyle, then God has an even more startling way of saying "You Dummy, I wasn't kidding." It's called death.

George Bernard Shaw put it well in *Mrs. Warren's Profession*: "People are always blaming their circumstances for what they are. I don't believe in circumstances. The people who get on in this world are the people who get up and look for circumstances they want, and if they can't find them, make them."

I hope you will do what you can to make next year even healthier. Remember that what counts most about your success is *how* you achieve it.

Workaholics

Workaholism? What can a psychologist from laid-back Southern California know about that? Well, you can believe that it's as common here as anywhere, and it's taking its toll day in and day out, especially among successful, achieving men and women between the ages of 30 and 50.

We've all heard of stories where the young lawyer or physician — after so many years of training, preparation and postponing life's pleasures — just gives it all up. One 43-year-old doctor told me, "All I ever do is work — when I'm not working, I go crazy." He recognized his problem and the price he and his family were paying. By doing so, he got what his family called their, "second chance." They were fortunate.

Try these questions to see where you or your loved one may be on the scale of workaholism.

(1) Are you highly competitive, hard-driving, intense and tied to your work?

(2) Do you use your work to get personal approval from others, when down deep inside you feel insecure?

(3) Are weekends and holidays just something you have to put up with until you can get back to work?

(4) Is your home simply another office?

(5) Do you take office equipment — dictating machines, calculators, telephones, pens and pads — with you wherever you go, even on vacations?

(6) Does work really make you happier than anything else in your life?

(7) Are sleep and leisure a waste of time in your view?

(8) Do you cut your vacations short (if you do take them — most workaholics don't) after a few days of restlessness?

(9) Are you suffering from irritability, fatigue, a lack of joy in your life, physical symptoms, social isolation?

If you answered yes to most of these, you're probably a workaholic. That's not all bad. Recent research has shown that many workaholics actually are quite happy and doing well. Those who are seem to have four factors that are associated with their successful workaholic lifestyles: (1) variety and independence in their work; (2) good health; (3) family support and acceptance; (4) a good fit between their personalities and their job demands.

For the not-so-fortunate majority of workaholics, the picture is radically different. Workaholics can be so focused on achievement status that they forget their human limits. Stress in their lives is met with — you guessed it — still harder work. This carries with it alienation and isolation from the joys of human life. Heart disease, family problems, ulcers, physical and emotional exhaustion, feelings of estrangement from their children — these are only a few of the costs of workaholism. It's an expensive and irrational trip.

So what can you do about it if you're already on the journey? If you're like many workaholics I've counseled, it may take serious family problems, illness or total burn-out to convince you of the need to radically alter your travel plans.

(1) Get a complete physical examination. Tuning into your body is always the *first* place to start.

(2) Ask yourself the question, "Am I doing what I *really* want?" It may be scary, but you've got to start with that kind of personal inventory.

(3) At work, set reasonable — not perfect — goals. Rid yourself of time-wasters. Say "no" more often. Make free time for yourself to enjoy your co-workers. Make your work environment as aesthetically pleasing as possible.

(4) If your work is mental, get some physical diversions. If it's physical work you do, play a quiet game or read in your spare time. Keep play as play. Some people do better with an external commitment — if that's you, get season tickets to the theatre or a sporting event. I also think it's critical to get away once in awhile for a weekend with your mate.

(5) Learn to relax with meditation or some other form of passive relaxation. You also ought to begin a weekly aerobic exercise program.

(6) Finally, if nothing you try seems to work, you may very well be a candidate for counseling. I know it's difficult to ask for help, but it's one sure sign of health.

Vacations: The Shortest Distance Between Two Paychecks

He complained, "All she wanted to do was shop, shop and shop some more!"

She countered, "And all he wanted to do was swim, smoke, scuba, play volleyball on the beach, and jog!"

Or another version: "I thought we were going to have a complete rest, just laying around the pool, and all my friend (or ex-friend!) wanted to do was non-stop sightseeing."

The environment makes no difference. Maui, Mexico or Morocco. The surprises, stress and strain of a vacation can ruin your trip faster than lost luggage.

Many folks believe, "If we just get away, everything will be great." But many who "need to get away from their problems" quickly discover that going away does not always make the big difference they looked forward to. Travel can be stressful even when things go well. But with jet lag, travel deadlines, reservations that fall through, new environments, foul weather, getting lost — traveling can be both a positive *and* negative experience.

First, problems just don't disappear. They remain for you when you return. Some recommend that it is important to prepare for your return before you set off by getting rid all of your work before you go so that your desk is clean when you come back. Get the refrigerator free of food that may be spoiled when you return and if you can't get the house totally clean, at least make sure that the bed has clean sheets on it waiting for you.

Second, since we typically create our own difficulties in life by our attitudes and views, we cannot take a vacation from ourselves. Our thoughts go with us wherever we go. It is important not to set yourself up to "fail." Focus your expectations on things that you can control while you're away, not on things that "could or should" happen.

Third, for some "Type A Workaholic" personalities, vacations are only seen as sources of stress.

Let's face it, for some people vacations really don't make any sense. They really don't. They get in a car, drive 550 miles, and what do they spend all their time looking for? A bed that feels just like home!

Some folks like to vacation abroad. It seems that today, thanks to modern jet travel, we can now be sick in countries we never even heard of before. Just keep in mind that your body will need to do some adjusting to new environments!

If you choose to travel with a friend or lover, life can get pretty complicated. It's important to understand each other's expectations for the time you will be away. Antiques or scenery? Sports or culture? Resting or running? Burger King or Le Plush Palace? First-class or coach? Window or aisle? Get together, in advance, and discuss your goals. Too many friendships can end as a result of poor vacation planning and mistaken assumptions.

It may sound cumbersome, but you must periodically assess how things are going with your travel companion. Being together 24 hours a day can lead to getting on each other's nerves. Be assertive, honest and willing to talk things out.

A mini vacation within a vacation — time away from each other for a short while — can be very helpful. Husbands and wives have difficulty accepting that idea at times, but a planned time-out can have an energizing effect on the relationship while you're on a trip.

It is also important to watch for your companion becoming too dependent on you, and vice-versa. Especially if you are experienced in traveling or have been to a place before, your friend may smother you out of anxiety, leaving you feeling responsible for your companion's good time.

Of course traveling with someone else doesn't have to be a negative experience. Companions can get close again, have time to talk about things that they've been putting off, let go of old roles, habits and routines, and relax with each other.

So, if you contemplate traveling with a companion, plan, get things off your chest while you're away, allow for each other's individuality, and you'll be more likely to remain friends when you return to the reality of home.

I recently took a group of 30 couples on a stress management and couples enrichment seminar to Maui. By planning for the pitfalls in advance, focusing on relationship enhancing experiences, building a time for individuals to explore their own interests, and preparing for re-entry into the home environment, all had a very enjoyable and meaningful time.

Incidentally, while everyone does it, it's better not to come home 15 minutes before you are expected to return to work. Leave yourself some time between vacation and your back-to-work routine. Unpack, go through the mail, and rest before going back to work. When you return from a vacation, if at all possible don't try to make up for the two weeks you were away in the first three days after you return.

A vacation ought to be a time to develop a new perspective on life. It ought to give you a chance to experience time in a way that's different than you usually experience it. And returning home ought not mean a rapid return to old habits, ways of thinking and routines. You can extend your vacation mentality with a code word, mental image, memento, or picture to remind you of "the way you were."

When all is said and done and the vacation is over, remember that you always have your pictures, slides, videotape, and souvenirs to look at. Did Kodak *invent* vacations?

Bon voyage and have a great trip!

Pink Slip Syndrome

Dear Dr. Mantell:

A few months ago, my husband was laid off. Since that time, he's become increasingly unbearable. He sleeps a lot, seems angry and frustrated all the time and has no patience anymore with the children. He just seems to have an all around bad attitude. He's even stopped looking for work. I'm at my wit's end. Is this normal for people who have lost their jobs? Please, any advice you may have would be appreciated.

Mrs. T

Dear Mrs. T:

"Normal" is one of those trigger words I try to stay away from. What your husband seems to be suffering from, though, is not uncommon. It's called the "Pink-Slip Syndrome," and it's no joy. Typical symptoms include low morale, anger and worry. Sadly, whenever our nation's unemployment rate increases, so does the psychological toll which accompanies the "pink-slip" — sometimes at a staggering rate.

Look at it from your husband's point of view. He was probably out there every day on time doing whatever he was asked to do. No doubt he worked hard, and didn't ask for favors. It wasn't his fault that his company suffered a financial set-back, decided to increase profits by reducing staff, or whatever it was that caused the lay off.

Perhaps he even saw it coming: a shortage of materials in the supply room, a crackdown against overtime, or just the recognition that there wasn't enough work for everyone to do. Or, like many of his co-workers, your husband may have closed his eyes to the warning signs of an impending lay-off. He may have been taken totally by surprise when the final word came.

People who suffer from the "Pink-Slip Syndrome" are generally affected on two levels. First, they know rationally that being laid off is not necessarily their fault, and so they blame a faulty system. However, on a deeper level, they do blame themselves.

You've probably heard your husband grumbling phrases like, "If only I had come to work a little earlier..." "If I hadn't taken that day off last December," or "I could have worked harder, longer, better..." Eventually, a sense of low self-worth may take hold. By then, the syndrome is full blown and characteristics appear like those you've described in your husband.

You can probably guess that the distress your husband is feeling makes it difficult for him to find work. It's not hard to spot individuals harboring hostility toward their old jobs and generally feeling lousy about themselves. No one wants to hire a depressed and angry person.

The problem can be serious. Social scientists have found that when unemployment rises 1 percent, 4.3 percent more men and 2.3 percent more women are admitted to state mental hospitals, and 4.1 percent more people kill themselves.

Until every pink slip carries a Surgeon General's warning that it may be "hazardous to your health," there are some things to watch for.

As you recognize with your husband's situation, usually the unemployed person is not the only one affected. His or her family, friends, co-workers and neighbors may all experience an increase in anxiety, depression or hostility. You may find your children's grades in school taking a nose dive. You've already felt the strain on your marriage.

While psychological counseling can't provide your husband with a job, it can help you and your husband cope more effectively with the situation. Sometimes just recognizing the relationship between losing one's job and physical and emotional stress can produce dramatic improvement.

Meanwhile, persistent efforts to find new employment — however frustrating — will help your husband to deal with the situation more effectively than staying home and moping. Lack of activity tends to exacerbate depression. Encourage (but don't nag) him to keep moving.

Anxiety, Panic and Fear

"Doctor, for the last several months I've been nervous and irritable; I break out in the sweats; I get jittery, my chest tightens and my heart pounds. My family doctor said it's my nerves and I need to see a psychologist." So begins the initial session of a young woman complaining about one of the most common disorders of our time — *anxiety*.

The symptoms of anxiety in its various forms raise havoc in the lives of millions of adults and children. It affects marriages, employment and general day-to-day functioning. Some people shun being in public places because of it, preferring instead to stay home where it is "safe" — where they will probably not experience an anxiety attack.

As with any emotional or medical disorder, the most effective treatment is based on a careful assessment and diagnosis of your specific kind of anxiety. The biology of your anxiety must also be understood to best determine whether or not medication is necessary, and if so, which one and how much is appropriate.

Until recently, many clinicians have satisfied themselves with a general approach to "bad nerves." How many times have you been told to, "slow down, give your nerves a rest?"

Let's take a look at five kinds of anxiety and their symptoms.

Panic Attacks

A spontaneous panic attack, unrelated to a specific event in your life, is like the body's alarm system going off for no apparent reason.

Palpitations, chest pain, smothering sensations, unsteady feelings, tingling in your hands and feet, butterflies in your stomach — these are some of the spontaneous symptoms. The sudden onset of feelings of fear, terror, or impending doom are quite typical of this sort of anxiety disorder.

Many find relief from the antidepressant medication imipramine, especially when the panic attack is associated with agoraphobia, another sort of anxiety. Psychotherapy, either individual or group, can also be highly effective when used in conjunction with medication or, in some cases, when used by itself. In cases where therapy is indicated, family-oriented counseling is usually well-advised to help family members understand the dysfunction.

Agoraphobia

This involves a generalized fear of being alone or of being in public places from which escape might be difficult. The panic attacks (often but not always associated with agoraphobia) may actually be a cause, in that some patients are so fearful of experiencing the panic attack they avoid going out at all. Crowds, busy streets, tunnels, bridges, and elevators are commonly avoided.

Again, psychotherapy, with or without medication for the panic attacks, is generally of use, especially when it includes training in relaxation and social skills.

Phobias

"Persistent and irrational fears of a specific object, activity or situation," is the general definition of a phobia. Agoraphobia is the most severe and pervasive of these disorders. Fear of dogs, cats, snakes, closed places (claustrophobia), and social embarrassment (social phobia) are also examples. Social and simple phobias not associated with panic disorders generally do well with behaviorally-oriented treatment in counseling.

Generalized Anxiety

The pop-psych term, "free-floating anxiety" best describes this group of symptoms for anxious patients. *Motor tension* — trembling, twitches, restlessness, easily startled; *Physical hyperactivity* — palpitations, sweating, dry mouth, dizziness, tingling; *Apprehension* — worry, anticipating doom; *Vigilance* — on edge, impatient. These are some of the common symptoms experienced by people whose anxiety seems unrelated to specific situations. They do not have panic attacks nor have they experienced a stressful life event or significant trauma. Generalized anxiety is felt more intensely than stress, and can be treated with appropriate medication and psychotherapy. Low self-esteem is often a contributing element.

Obsessive-Compulsive Disorders

If anxiety is associated with being unable to complete a specific compulsive ritual, such as hand-washing, or is associated with a recurrent, persistent thought you cannot ignore, the condition may be categorized as an obsessive-compulsive behavior disorder. There are generally no panic attacks; medication, along with psychotherapy, has been found to be of use.

Despite common mythology, obsessive-compulsive anxiety sufferers do *not* enjoy the activity — though it provides some tension relief.

Thoughts of violence, contamination and doubt are the common obsessions. Counting, checking, touching and hand-washing are the commonly seen compulsions.

As you can see, anxiety has many faces; it's not a simple matter of "bad nerves." With more careful classification, managing anxiety more effectively becomes that much easier. Of course, it's a tense world. But no one should suffer needlessly. Proper evaluation and treatment of the anxiety disorders is readily available.

"I Can't Stand the Pressure"

Whether it's a business investment, the stock market, school grades, physical health or your love life, now and then everyone panics.

Anxiety is a normal emotional reaction to irrational, distorted and unrealistic interpretations of life's situations. Whether you overestimate danger, or underestimate your ability to respond to your perceived danger, tension and anxiety may very likely result. The feeling of helplessness that goes along with exaggerated fear can be emotionally crippling.

Gary Emery, Ph.D., and James Campbell, M.D., co-authored the book, *Rapid Relief From Emotional Distress,* which I recommend for anyone who suffers from panic and anxiety symptoms. Here are some extremely helpful ideas from their book:

• Jot down three situations you have experienced recently that created anxiety for you. Study the list to determine how your *need to control* something caused you to become anxious or worried. The antidote is to change the feeling of being helpless to control situations into situations in which you have some choice. Statements such as "I can't stand it," "I must get out of the situation," "I must get them to change the way they react to me," are all examples of situations where you are creating tension by demanding control.

• Whenever I feel a bit anxious before giving a public talk or appearing on radio or television, I *accept my anxiety* by announcing to whoever is around "I'm feeling a little anxious right now." This, instead of trying to cover it over, allows me to deal with it better.

• Drs. Emery and Campbell suggest that you use *positive self-thoughts* rather than negative and irrational ones. This may include "stay calm," instead of "don't be nervous." The anxiety experts also suggest that you use self-awareness techniques not only when you're feeling tense and anxious but also when you're feeling calm and in a stable mind set. Writing things down in a self-help diary is extremely helpful. Many of the patients that I treat in my office for anxiety find that self-monitoring gives them a sense of control over their anxiety.

• Certainly *exercise* can be very valuable in the treatment of emotional distress. The most common exercise of all, walking, is easy to do and a great stress reducer. Jogging, aerobic dance, swimming, and jumping rope use adrenalin in a positive way and help reduce stress and tension. Just as verbal catharsis can be useful in reducing stress, physical catharsis is also important.

For many people, anxiety may seem to be a way of life; it does not have to be. Does medication — such as Valium and other tranquilizers — seem to be the quick and easy way to reduce stress and tension? You'll pay long term costs by dealing with anxiety that way. Unless the anxiety is debilitating and your physician recommends it, stay away from these medications. Under the watchful eye of a psychiatrist or physician, these medications can be a valuable aid in reducing anxiety and making it more manageable, *if coupled with appropriate psychotherapy and counseling.*

Anxiety does not have to be a great stumbling block in your life; brief counseling and self-help skills can accomplish a great deal. Try Emery and Campbell's approaches. If anxiety continues to be a problem for you, consult your physician or a mental health professional.

Want to Go Crazy?

It's simple. Find *"The Best"* of anything.

Here's a current example: If you really want to ensure that you'll go so far off the deep end that you may never come back, buy "THE BEST" computer. Sure I know this book is supposed to be of help to you... to help you *not* go "mishuga." But having recently survived (barely) the purchase of a computer system, I had to write about a new syndrome I stumbled on. It's called "IBM": "I Become Mental." (In yiddish, "I Become Mishuga.")

Let's face it. Computers are essential today. After all, they have saved millions and millions of human-hours — of course we need those hours to straighten out all the mistakes computers have added to our lives!

Computer salespeople can really get to you. Before you know it, they can actually have you believing that you found "THE BEST" computer. But it's funny — after you have spent sixteen thousand hours of research, twelve hundred hours shopping, and twice as much time in sweat-filled decision-making, finally made up your mind and made the big purchase — you overhear the salesperson next to you tell *his* customer what's wrong with the system you just spent eight thousand dollars on.

What is this elusive "best" everyone else seems to have? Just listen to people discussing vacation sites, cars, interior decorators, stereos, hairdressers, doctors, computers and, of course, restaurants. Who doesn't know "The Best" pizzeria, Chinese restaurant, or sushi bar in any city in the United States? You don't, that's who! How do I know? Because all you have to do is ask the "other guy," and he'll gladly tell you *he* knows "The Best."

It is truly amazing that people invest so much of their precious time on this earth trying to convince "the other guy" that they know what's "Best." As if there were such a thing.

So what is this mania with "The Best"? More often than not a cover — for feeling "The Worst." Here is a general rule of thumb: the more someone tries to convince you that she has "The Best," the more insecure she feels about herself in relation to you. So why argue with her? You'll only make her more defensive, which will only make her try harder to convince you.

Whew! What a vicious circle. If you continue to try to convince someone "your" pizzeria is better, following my rule of thumb, you feel worse about yourself than that person does about him- or herself. Then we have two people, arguing for what is absolutely an impossible outcome — whose is *best*?

I want to suggest a different concept to you that will certainly make your life easier, less complicated, less stressful, and more decisive. It's called *"Good Enough."* The next time your "friend" shouts to you, "No way, that Chinese restaurant isn't nearly as good as the one I go to," simply say, "That may be, but for me it's good enough."

Now I'm not suggesting you passively settle for something you know is second rate — God forbid you ever settle for something. No, I'm recommending you put life in its proper perspective. If you like something, someone, or someplace and someone else says it's not "The Best," so what? *You* liked it, remember? For you, it was "good enough."

The perfect marriage doesn't exist. The perfect child doesn't exist. And the perfect computer doesn't exist. So why do people try to convince you of the perfect — "The Best" — tennis racket, compact disc player, school, dentist, or kitchen design plan? I believe it has a lot to do with their delusion that there is actually such a thing and they — chosen as they are — have it.

But of course it is an illusion, all too often aimed at helping them feel better about themselves. "Since I can recommend 'The Best' wine for dinner, I am somehow a better person." A sad illusion, but all too common.

Stop neurotically driving yourself and others around you for perfection. You won't achieve it. Do *your* best, certainly, but relax about being "*The* Best." There is no such thing.

When I realized I wasn't buying "The Best" computer, I was no longer addicted. I was able to buy one that was "good enough." Do you hear the difference?

You will reduce the pressure in your life, minimize stress and tension when you begin applying the concept of "good enough." It will help you let go and enjoy more of your life. What more could you want? Something better? No, that's good enough.

'Tis the Season to be...Stressed?

For the average person, the holiday season carries so many changes in feelings that it makes Disneyland's Space Mountain look tame. Whether you get emotionally high and stay up until after New Year's Day, fall into the pits of depression and slowly climb your way out by Valentine's Day, or go up and down on the emotional roller-coaster, holiday time generally means stress.

Stress is unavoidable at any time, but it seems for many it is especially so from November to January. Stress is a normal reaction to any demand made upon you. Holiday demands are often so great that stress seems to have become a common part of holiday celebrations. It's as if you are somehow "strange" if you *don't* complain about being under tension. And if you actually enjoy the holiday season, well, you may be looked at with even more suspicion.

My experience suggests that, contrary to popular beliefs, Thanksgiving and Christmas are NOT the times for increased numbers of suicides. In fact, December is the lowest suicide month of the year, with suicides reaching a peak in the spring.

So what does all this talk about holiday stress mean? Why does this time of year set many people into emotional turmoil? And more importantly, what can you do about it?

If you have walked through any shopping center within the last several weeks, you may be amazed at the "total push" effort designed to take money out of your pockets and put it into someone else's. To live on an average American salary in these days of intense inflation is tough enough. But to take that income and try to stretch it for life's luxuries such as personal computers, digital watches, big-screen T.V.'s, video cassette tape recorders and other holiday "lures," may be next to impossible. It's difficult enough to recognize that you may not be able to afford some of the luxuries of life during the year, but during the holiday season when the gift list mounts, the pressure may be inescapable.

Explaining to your husband, wife, or children that you just can't afford something should be rather straightforward. But it becomes impossible for people with unrealistic expectations.

I recommend that as soon into the holiday season as possible you sit down with your family and discuss a budget you can live with into January and the new year. Include your youngsters as well, down to the age of about seven years. Plan ahead for your spending rather than choking yourselves for the rest of the year.

One family I worked with not long ago told me of a Chanukah tradition that they have which helps cut down on the holiday expenditures: they give prizes for whoever *makes* the most creative gift. This serves to bring the family together and helps reduce stress on the bread winners.

You might find it helpful to stay out of the stores. Of course, in today's marketing world, so many stores send catalogs right into your home that the simple process of opening your mail can become stressful. Above all, avoid the addiction to *things*.

Law enforcement officials, restaurant staff, and other service workers often have to work over holidays. If this conflicts with religious, family, or personal beliefs it surely may create additional stress. There is nothing wrong with celebrating a holiday when you are able to. I can certainly recall veterans celebrating holidays, birthdays and other key celebrations when they came home — often long after the ''official'' date. Be sure the family understands (if it's true) that you would prefer to be at home with your family. Nevertheless, you have a responsibility to which you must adhere.

One officer told me that he actually looked forward to going off to work to avoid all of the fuss that goes along with Christmastime at his household. I guess this supports the notion that stress is based on your reaction to an event rather than the event itself. For one person "missing the holiday" by having to work may mean misery; for another it may mean happiness.

What do holiday celebrations mean? Many look at them as a "time-out" from day-to-day cares and a "time-in" for recalling larger, more permanent truths. While this view may be accurate, the holidays also provide the seeds for stress and depression. If you have recently lost a spouse or other loved one through death or divorce, or your children have grown up and moved away, the holiday season will bring memories — good or bad — of earlier holidays. Those who are not able to be with their families find separation to be the most stressful part of the season.

Most of us recall vividly and warmly earlier holiday seasons and celebrations when we were children, taken care of and provided for. Things certainly have changed! Now we are no longer the carefree children but the responsible adults; caring for others adds a measure of stress at this time of the year.

Holiday celebrations are times for friends and family members to renew relationships. Time and effort spent together — cooking, baking, gift-shopping and buying — provide many chances to say "I care." Beyond the everyday opportunities to express those positive feelings, the holidays have come to symbolize that, "despite it all, I'll be there for you."

Great expectations around what a holiday celebration "should" be like can be most upsetting and disappointing. We come to look upon the holiday time as the perfect celebration, in the image of Norman Rockwell, if you will. For many people, depression — the sense of hopelessness, helplessness, and worthlessness — rests on the fact that you are comparing what you feel should be with what is. The greater the disparity, the greater the depression. Giving up expectations that others have of you, whether about gift-giving or the type of celebration, will go a long way in diminishing holiday blues.

For some of you who are having marital or family problems, the holiday season may bring those difficulties into even clearer focus as you compare what *is* to what you think should be. Seeing television and magazine advertisements of perfectly groomed and attired upper middle-class people celebrating by a magnificent fireplace — while your marriage or family is turning sour — can be difficult. The expectations that you set up, that this will be a perfect Christmas or Thanksgiving, only sets everyone up for disappointment. Stop measuring yourself against what you have idealized, and instead concentrate on what's real, present, and available now.

If you go into the holiday season with low self-esteem, and feeling as though too much is expected from you, it's quite tough: too much may be expected from people who feel they have too little to give. It is more than difficult, frankly impossible, for one's own life to live up to a Norman Rockwell image of home and hearth.

Remember that you are just human, and there is no such thing as a perfect celebration.

Forgiving and Becoming

An 85-year-old man who learned he was dying wrote a classic reflection, which has been widely quoted:

If I had my life to live over again, I'd try to make more mistakes next time. I wouldn't try to be so perfect. I would relax more. I'd limber up. I'd be sillier than I've been on this trip. In fact, I know very few things that I would take so seriously. I'd be crazier. I'd be less hypnotic. I'd take more chances, I'd take more trips. I'd climb more mountains, I'd swim more rivers, I'd watch more sunsets, I'd go more places I've never been to. I'd eat more ice cream and fewer beans.

I'd have more actual troubles and fewer imaginary ones. You see, I was one of those people who lived prophylactically and sensibly hour after hour and day after day. Oh, I've had my moments, and if I had it to do all over again, I'd have more of those moments. In fact, I'd try to have nothing but beautiful moments — moment by moment by moment.

I've been one of those people who never went anywhere without a thermometer, a hot water bottle, a gargle, a raincoat and a parachute. If I had it to do all over again, I'd travel lighter next time.

If I had it to do all over again, I'd start barefoot earlier in the spring and stay that way later in the fall. I'd ride more merry-go-rounds, I'd watch more sunrises and I'd play with more children, if I had my life to live over again. But you see, I don't.''

This is a rather lengthy quote, but I believe it makes a beautiful point. Keep life in perspective. Take emotional inventory of where you've been and where you're going. What's important — really important — to you? If your answer differs significantly from the way you fill up your life now, do something about it, NOW!

Don't spend time crying about what happened yesterday — the love you lost, the business that didn't make it, the dreams that didn't pan out, the unfinished business of life — these are part of history. Yesterday is over with!

Let go of the past so you can live more fully now. The only way I know that you can "change the past" is by acting different *now;* you can change tomorrow's past by changing today.

How much excess emotional baggage do you carry with you from yesterday to today to tomorrow? Past grudges, hurts, gripes? Let them go, just once, and see how much easier it is to enjoy life. Are you willing to forgive, stop blaming, release, forget and say, "It's O.K."?

After all, people are only fallible human beings who goof — and that includes you. Fight the idea that if someone mistreats you, you *must* see it as horrible and unbearable — that therefore the person must be seen as an *utterly bad person.*

It's been said that accepting things and people as they are is not surrender, but rather, liberation. When you refuse to let go of a past hurt, you condemn yourself to treading emotional water forever. It's as though a piece of your energy will always be bound up in negativity. When you let go, you cut the emotional weights around your neck.

What a freeing experience to let go, to start anew, to begin living *your* life as you want to. Without the emotional binds, without the wasted energy, without giving your power to the past.

Eugene O'Neill wrote that, "None of us can heal the things that life has done to us. They're done before we can realize what's being done, and they then make you do things all your life until these things are constantly coming between you and what you'd like to be. And in that way you seem to lose yourself forever."

By holding on, not letting go, expending wasted energy, you can't really be you. And as Elie Weisel wrote in *Souls on*

Fire: "When we die and we go to heaven, and we meet our Maker, our Maker is not going to say to us, 'Why didn't you become a messiah? Why didn't you discover a cure for such and such?' The only thing we're going to be asked at that precious moment is, 'Why didn't you become *you*?'"

Choosing a Therapist: A Mensch is a Mensch

You've tried everything. Vacations, relaxation, slowing down — even speeding up. You know counseling or psychotherapy is necessary — your physician has recommended it for some time — but you've avoided it, thinking the problem will go away by itself. It hasn't.

You now recognize the need for help and are left with a question. Who do I go to? You've read horror stories in the paper about therapists who do everything from sleep with their patients to having them scream naked in a group of other folks with personal problems.

So, how do you choose a therapist that can help you?

Research completed at Northwestern University's Department of Psychology attempted to answer that very question. When seeking therapy, most people will ask a friend for a recommendation. Many talk with their physician, lawyer, school guidance counselor or clergy. A small number let their "fingers do the walking" and select one at random from the phone book. The latter is *not* the best method.

You certainly want a therapist who can help you work on your problem without you having to spend time or money overcoming impediments to the therapeutic relationship.

According to the Northwestern research, you will know if you have chosen the right therapist after your initial telephone call if the therapist:
* seems attentive and listens to what you are saying
* seems to understand how you think and feel
* communicates respect for you
* thinks your feelings are valid and gives reasonable responses to the problems you are dealing with
* communicates a sense of optimism — that he or she is competent to help with your problem.

Harvard Medical School researchers took a different approach. They reviewed therapists' concerns in searching for *their own* therapists. Avoiding "therapists who were associated with them personally or professionally," they sought a therapist who:
* had a reputation for competence
* seemed warm and caring
* appeared to respect them
* was interested, understanding and warm
* was willing to talk, to be responsive.

The Northwestern and Harvard studies suggest that the therapist qualifications desired by therapists themselves are no different from those of non-professionals when they seek help.

Some research points to the possibility of a better therapeutic bond forming if the therapist is the same sex and in the same birth order as the client. In essence, the more similarities, the better.

Therapists and non-therapists alike use all available cues in deciding on who to go to for professional help. In the Harvard research, believe it or not, the health of the therapist's plants and the style of his or her clothes were significant, though superficial, cues to which therapists paid attention in choosing their own doctor.

So how do *you* choose your therapist? Follow some of the guidelines described above. Choose someone you like, appreciate and respect. Someone who helps you feel affirmed, appreciated and respected. You'll probably feel more comfortable with a therapist who is appropriately warm, active and expressive.

By contacting local professional societies, universities, and talking with physicians, counselors, clergy, you can get a fairly good idea of a particular individual's reputation for competence. By all means don't be afraid to ask questions of your potential therapist to ascertain, on your own, his or her level of expertise and experience. An ethical professional will explain his or her approach, discuss specific techniques which may be employed, and answer your questions frankly. It is very appropriate to clarify the fee schedule in advance, also.

Choosing a therapist is a critical decision that should not be made blindly. If you have doubts, talk it over with the therapist. Mis-matches sometimes occur and can be rectified by a referral to another therapist.

Perhaps the best piece of advice is the most difficult to explain — if the therapist you choose is a ''mensch,'' congratulations. That may be the best sign for a productive therapeutic relationship.

References

YOU

Alberti, Robert E., and Emmons, Michael L., *Your Perfect Right* (fifth edition). San Luis Obispo, CA: Impact Publishers, 1986.

Benson, Herbert, and Miriam Klipper, *The Relaxation Response*. New York: Avon Books, 1976.

Berne, Eric, *What Do You Say After You Say Hello?*. New York: Bantam Books, 1975.

Branden, Nathaniel, *The Disowned Self*. New York: Bantam Books, 1973.

Cooper, Kenneth. *Total Well-Being*. New York: Bantam Books, 1972.

Cousins, Norman. *The Healing Heart: Antidotes to Panic and Helplessness*. New York: Norton, 1983.

Dyer, Wayne, *Pulling Your Own Strings*. New York: Avon Books, 1979.

Ellis, Albert and Robert Harper, *A New Guide to Rational Living*. New York: Institute for Rational-Emotive Therapy.

Fensterheim, Herbert, and Jean Baer, *Stop Running Scared*. New York: Dell Publishing Co., 1978.

Harris, Thomas, *I'm OK, You're OK*. New York: Avon Books, 1982.

Maltz, Maxwell, *Psychocybernetics and Self-Fulfillment*. New York: Bantam Books, 1973.

Satir, Virginia, *Peoplemaking*. Palo Alto, CA: Science and Behavior Books, 1972.

Sheehy, Gail, *Passages*. New York: Bantam Books, 1977.

Zimbardo, Phillip, *Shyness*. New York: Jove Publications, 1987.

YOUR RELATIONSHIPS

Bach, George, and Peter Wyden, *The Intimate Enemy: How to Fight Fair in Love and Marriage*. New York: Avon Books, 1981.

Campbell, Susan, *The Couple's Journey*. San Luis Obispo, CA: Impact Publishers, 1980.

Comfort, Alex, *The Joy of Sex*. New York: Fireside, 1972, 1985.

Gibran, Khalil. *The Prophet*. New York: Alfred A. Knopf, Inc., 1984.

Lasswell, Marcia and Norman Lobsenz, *No Fault Marriage*. New York: Ballantine, 1977.

Lazarus, Arnold, *Marital Myths*. San Luis Obispo, CA: Impact Publishers, 1985.

Levenson, Sam. *You Don't Have to be in Who's Who to Know What's What*. New York: Simon & Schuster Inc., 1982.

Otto, Herbert A. and Roberta, *Total Sex*. New York: Signet.

Powell, John, *Why Am I Afraid to Tell You Who I Am?* Allen, TX: Argus Communications, 1979.

Rogers, Carl R., *Becoming Partners*. New York: Delta, 1973.

Taylor, Anita and Robert, *Couples: The Art of Staying Together*. New York: Acropolis, 1980.

Zunin, Leonard and Natalie, *Contact: The First Four Minutes*. New York: Ballantine, 1975.

Organizations:

Sex Information and Education Council of the United States, 84 5th Avenue, Suite #407, New York, NY 10011.

YOUR FAMILY

CHILDREN/PARENTING

Csikszentmihalyi, Mihaly and Reed Larson, *Being Adolescent: Conflict and Growth in the Teen-Age Years*. New York: Basic Books, 1984.

Bedford, Stewart. *Instant Replay*. New York: Institute For Rational-Emotive Therapy, Inc., 1974.

Boston Women's Health Book Collective, *Ourselves, Our Children*. New York: Random House, 1978

Dinkmeyer, Don, *Systematic Training for Effective Parenting*. Circle Pines, MN: American Guidance Service, 1983.

Dodson, Fitzhugh, *How To Parent*. New York: Signet, 1973.

Eimers, Robert and Robert Aitcheson, *Effective Parents, Responsible Children*. New York: McGraw Hill, 1977.

Ernst, K. *Danny and His Thumb*. Spokane, WA: Treehouse Productions, 1973.

Fassler, J. *Don't Worry Bear*. New York: Human Sciences Press, 1971.

Gordon, Thomas, *Parent Effectiveness Training*. New York: New American Library, 1975.

Gross, Leonard H. *The Parent's Guide to Teenagers*. New York: Macmillan Publishing Company, 1981.

Hagstrom, Julie, and Morrill, Joan. *Games Babies Play* and *More Games Babies Play*. New York: Pocket Books, 1983.

Levi, Miriam. *Effective Jewish Parenting*. Feldheim Publishers, 1986.

Shapiro, Jerrold Lee, *When Men Are Pregnant*. San Luis Obispo, CA: Impact Publishers, 1987.

Smith, Sally L., *No Easy Answers: The Learning Disabled Child*. New York: Bantam Books, 1981.

Spock, Benjamin. *Baby & Child Care*. New York: Pocket Books, 1982.

Wahlroos, Sven, *Family Communication*. New York: New American Library, 1983.

Winn, Marie. *Children Without Childhood*. New York: Pantheon Books, 1983.

Organizations:

American Academy of Pediatrics, 1801 Hinman Avenue, Evanston, IL 60204.

American Association for Marriage & Family Therapy, 1717 K Street N. W., Washington, D.C. 20006.

American Society for Adolescent Psychiatry, 24 Green Valley Road, Wallingford, PA 19086.

Council for Exceptional Children, 1920 Association Drive, Reston, VA 22091.

Gifted Education Specialists, Office of Elementary and Secondary Education, Donahue Building, Room 1725-A, 400 Maryland Avenue, S.W., Washington, D.C. 20202.

DIVORCE/SINGLE PARENTING

Fisher, Bruce, *Rebuilding: When Your Relationship Ends*. San Luis Obispo, CA: Impact Publishers, 1981.

Gardner, Richard, *The Boys and Girls Book About Divorce*. New York: Bantam Books, 1971.

Krantzler, Mel, *Creative Divorce*. New York: Signet, 1975.

Satir, Virginia, et al. *Helping Families to Change*. New York: Jason Aronson, 1976.

Visher, Emily and John, *Step-Families*. New York: Brunner-Mazel, 1979.

Wallerstein, Judith S. and Kelly, Joan Berlin. *Surviving the Breakup: How Children and Parents Cope with Divorce*. New York: Basic Books, 1982.

Organizations:

Association of Family and Conciliation Courts, 2680 Southwest Glen Eagles Road, Lake Oswego, OR 97304.

Family Mediation Association, 2380 S.W., 34 Way, Fort Lauderdale, FL 33312.

Parents Without Partners, 7910 Woodmont Avenue, Suite #1000, Washington, D.C. 20014.

AGING

Gardner, David L., and Beatty, Grace J. *Stop Stress and Aging Now*. Windham, NH: American Training and Research Associates Publishers, 1985.

Silverstone, Barbara, and Hyman, Helen Kandel. *You and Your Aging Parent*. New York: Pantheon Books, 1982.

Uris, Auren. *Over Fifty*. New York: Bantam Books, 1981.

Organizations:
American Geriatrics Society, 10 Columbus Circle, New York, NY
   10019.
Grey Panthers, 3635 Chestnut Street, Philadelphia, PA 19104.
National Council of Senior Citizens, 1511 'K' Street N.W.,
   Washington, D.C. 20005.

THERAPY

Burns, David, *Feeling Good: The New Mood Therapy.* New York:
   Morrow, 1980.
Herink, Richie, *The Psychotherapy Handbook.* New York: Meridian
   (NAL), 1980.
Satir, Virginia, *Conjoint Family Therapy.* Palo Alto, CA: Science and
   Behavior Books, 1982.
Stuart, Richard B., *Helping Couples Change.* New York: Guilford
   Press, 1980.

YOUR HEALTH

DIET/EXERCISE

Burns, David D., *Intimate Connections.* New York: William Morrow &
   Company, Inc., 1985.
Friedman, Meyer, and Rosenman, Ray, *Type A Behavior and Your
   Heart,* New York: Knopf, 1974.
Morehouse, Lawrence, and Gross, Leonard. *Total Fitness in Thirty
   Minutes a Week.* New York: Pocket Books, 1987.
Sheehan, George. *This Running Life.* New York: Simon & Schuster,
   1981.
Stuart, Richard, *Act Thin: Stay Thin.* New York: Jove   Publications,
   1987.

Organizations:
American College of Sports Medicine. 1440 Monroe Street, Madison,
   WI 53206.

ALCOHOL/DRUGS

Hazelden Educational Publications, *Teen Drug Use: What Can Parents
   Do?* Center City, MN: Hazelden.
Johnson, Vernon, *I'll Quit Tomorrow.* New York: Harper & Row, 1980.
McKean, Margaret, *The Stop Smoking Book.* San Luis Obispo, CA:
   Impact Publishers, 1987.

National Council on Alcoholism, *When Your Teenager Starts Drinking*. New York: NCA (733 Third Avenue, 10017).

Steiner, Claude, *Games Alcoholics Play*. New York: Ballantine, 1977.

Organizations:

Bay Haven Treatment Program, Samaritan Health Center, 713 Ninth Street, Bay City, MI 48708. (517) 894-3799.

Hazelden Outreach Services, Box 11, Center City, MN 55012.

DEPRESSION

Bloomfield, Harold, and Robert Kory: *Inner Joy*. New York: Jove Publications, 1985.

Kline, Nathan. *From Sad to Glad*. New York: Ballantine Books, 1981.

Kline, Nathan (editor). *Factors in Depression*. New York: Raven Press, 1974.

Organizations:

Mental Health Clearing House, National Institute of Mental Health, U.S. Department of Health & Human Services, 5600 Fishers Lane, Rockville, MD 20857.

American Psychological Association, 1200 17th Street, N.W., Washington, D.C. 20036.

DEATH/DYING

Colgrove, Melba, Bloomfield, Harold, and Peter McWilliams, *How to Survive the Loss of a Love*. New York: Bantam Books, 1977.

Fassler, Joan. *My Grandpa Died Today*. New York: Human Sciences Press, Inc., 1983.

Kubler-Ross, Elizabeth, *On Death and Dying*. New York: MacMillan, 1970.

Loewinsohn, R.J. *Survival Handbook for Widows*. New York: American Association of Retired Persons, 1984.

...AND THE REST OF YOUR LIFE

Berne, Eric, *A Layman's Guide to Psychiatry and Psychoanalysis*. New York: Ballantine, 1982.

Bolles, Richard Nelson, *What Color Is Your Parachute?*. Berkeley, CA: Ten Speed Press, 1988 (revised annually).

Cooper, Cary L. *The Stress Check: Coping with the Stresses of Life and Work*. Englewood Cliffs, NJ: Prentice-Hall, 1980.

Dyer, Wayne, *Your Erroneous Zones*. New York: Avon Books, 1977.

Emery, Gary, and James Campbell, *Rapid Relief from Emotional Distress*. New York: Fawcett, 1987.

Rosten, Leo, *The Joys of Yiddish*. New York: Washington Square Press, 1970.

Wiesel, Elie, *Souls on Fire*. New York: Summit Books, 1982.

Organizations:

American Academy of Stress Disorders, 8 South Michigan Avenue, Chicagò, IL 60603.

Catalyst, 14 E. 60th Street, New York, NY 10022.

Index

. . . more books with "IMPACT"

BEYOND THE POWER STRUGGLE
Dealing With Conflict in Love and Work
by Susan M. Campbell, Ph.D.

Explores relationship issues from the viewpoint that, "Differences are inevitable, but conflict and struggle are not." Helps expand perspectives on relationships in love and at work. Psychologist Campbell challenges us to see both sides of a conflict by seeing both sides of ourselves. ("Power struggles **between** people generally mirror the power struggles **within** themselves.") A creative and thoughtful analysis, accompanied by specific exercises to help relationships grow.
Softcover $8.95   Book No. 46-1

NO IS NOT ENOUGH
Helping Teenagers Avoid Sexual Assault
by Caren Adams, Jennifer Fay and Jan Loreen-Martin

Guidebook for parents provides proven, realistic strategies to help teens avoid victimization: acquaintance rape, exploitation by adults, touching, influence of media, peer pressures. Includes a primer on **what** to say and **when**. Tells how to provide teens with information they need to recognize compromising situations and skills they need to resist pressure.
Softcover $6.95   Book No. 35-6

WORKING FOR PEACE: A Handbook of Practical Psychology And Other Tools
Neil Wollman, Ph.D., Editor

Thirty-five chapter collection of guidelines, ideas and suggestions for improving effectiveness of peace work activities for individuals and groups. Written by psychologists and other experts in communication, speech, and political science.
Softcover $9.95   Book No. 37-2

MARITAL MYTHS: Two Dozen Mistaken Beliefs That Can Ruin A Marriage [Or Make A Bad One Worse]
by Arnold A. Lazarus, Ph.D.

Twenty-four myths of marriage are exploded by a world-renowned psychologist/marital therapist who has treated hundreds of relationships in over 25 years of practice. Full of practical examples and guidance for self-help readers who want to improve their own marriages.
Softcover $6.95   Book No. 51-8

WHEN MEN ARE PREGNANT
Needs and Concerns of Expectant Fathers
by Jerrold Lee Shapiro, Ph.D.

The first in-depth guide for men who are "expecting." Based on interviews with over 200 new fathers. Covers the baby decision, stages of pregnancy, physical and emotional factors, childbirth, and the first six weeks of fatherhood.
Softcover $8.95   Book No. 62-3

COMMUNITY DREAMS: Ideas for Enriching Neighborhood and Community Life
by Bill Berkowitz, Ph.D.

A unique collection of ideas for enriching neighborhood and community life. Hundreds of fresh, practical suggestions on street life, transportation, housing, festivals, recreation, employment, beautification, families, traditions, skills, food, economic development, energy, health, agencies, support groups, parks, media, workplaces and much more.
Softcover $8.95   Book No. 29-1

WHAT DO I DO WHEN...? A Handbook for Parents and Other Beleaguered Adults
by Juliet V. Allen, M.A.

"A parent's hotline in handbook." Ready-reference answers to over 50 childrearing dilemmas. Comprehensive, practical, common-sense solutions that **really work.** Short on theory, long on practical solutions to crying, fighting, bedwetting, car behavior, self-esteem, shyness, working parents, discipline, and much, much more.
Softcover $8.95   Book No. 23-2

TRUST YOURSELF— You Have The Power: A Holistic Handbook for Self-Reliance
by Tony Larsen, D. Min.

Dr. Larsen, teacher, counselor and Unitarian-Universalist minister, demonstrates how each of us has the power to handle our world. This can be done in a completely natural way and depends only upon the power which we already possess.
Softcover $8.95   Book No. 18-6

SHOPPER'S GUIDE TO THE MEDICAL MARKETPLACE
by Robert B. Keet, M.D., and Mary Nelson, M.S.

Answers to your health care questions, and a "map" for finding your way through the maze of physicians, hospitals, clinics, insurance, tests, medications, and other services in the "medical marketplace." Explains technology and procedures. Sample questionnaires and checklists help you get the information you need for good decision making.
Softcover $11.95   8" x 10"   Book No. 52-6

YOUR PERFECT WRITE: The Manual For Self-Help Writers
by Robert E. Alberti, Ph.D.

Psychologist, publisher, and co-author of 660,000-copy popular psychology book, **Your Perfect Right,** offers practical advice on writing style, subject matter, organization, working with editors and publishers, financial matters, more. Particularly valuable for human service professionals "translating" behavioral science jargon for popular markets.
Softcover $9.95   Book No. 40-2

GETTING APART TOGETHER: The Couple's Guide to a Fair Divorce or Separation
by Martin Kranitz, M.A.

Couples can save time, money, heartache by preparing their own fair settlement **before they see an attorney.** Procedures for cooperative negotiation of co-parenting, custody, property, support, insurance, finances, taxes. Includes agendas, forms.
Softcover $8.95   Book. No. 58-5

SEND FOR OUR FREE CATALOG

Impact Publishers' books are available at booksellers throughout the U.S.A. and in many other countries. If you are not able to find a title of interest at a nearby bookstore, we would be happy to fill your direct order. Please send us:
1. Complete name, address and zip code information
2. The full title and book no.'s of the book(s) you want
3. The number of copies of each book
4. California residents add 6% sales tax
5. Add $2.25 shipping for the first book; $.25 for each additional book
VISA or MasterCard are acceptable; be sure to include complete card number, expiration date, and your authorizing signature.
Prices effective August, 1988, and subject to change without notice.
Send your order to: **Impact 🐌 Publishers**

P.O. Box 1094, San Luis Obispo, CA 93406

[805] 543-5911